THE TREATISE ON THE ELUCIDATION OF THE KNOWABLE

THE CYCLE OF THE FORMATION OF THE SCHISMATIC DOCTRINES

BDK English Tripiṭaka 61-VI, 76-I

THE TREATISE ON THE ELUCIDATION OF THE KNOWABLE

Translated from the Chinese
(Taishō Volume 32, Number 1645)

by

Charles Willemen

THE CYCLE OF THE FORMATION OF THE SCHISMATIC DOCTRINES

Translated from the Chinese
(Taishō Volume 49, Number 2031)

by

TSUKAMOTO Keishō

Numata Center
for Buddhist Translation and Research
2004

First Printing, 2004
ISBN: 1-886439-30-3
Library of Congress Catalog Card Number: 2004107180

Published by
Numata Center for Buddhist Translation and Research
2620 Warring Street
Berkeley, California 94704

Printed in the United States of America

A Message on the Publication of the English Tripiṭaka

The Buddhist canon is said to contain eighty-four thousand different teachings. I believe that this is because the Buddha's basic approach was to prescribe a different treatment for every spiritual ailment, much as a doctor prescribes a different medicine for every medical ailment. Thus his teachings were always appropriate for the particular suffering individual and for the time at which the teaching was given, and over the ages not one of his prescriptions has failed to relieve the suffering to which it was addressed.

Ever since the Buddha's Great Demise over twenty-five hundred years ago, his message of wisdom and compassion has spread throughout the world. Yet no one has ever attempted to translate the entire Buddhist canon into English throughout the history of Japan. It is my greatest wish to see this done and to make the translations available to the many English-speaking people who have never had the opportunity to learn about the Buddha's teachings.

Of course, it would be impossible to translate all of the Buddha's eighty-four thousand teachings in a few years. I have, therefore, had one hundred thirty-nine of the scriptural texts in the prodigious Taishō edition of the Chinese Buddhist canon selected for inclusion in the First Series of this translation project.

It is in the nature of this undertaking that the results are bound to be criticized. Nonetheless, I am convinced that unless someone takes it upon himself or herself to initiate this project, it will never be done. At the same time, I hope that an improved, revised edition will appear in the future.

It is most gratifying that, thanks to the efforts of more than a hundred Buddhist scholars from the East and the West, this monumental project has finally gotten off the ground. May the rays of the Wisdom of the Compassionate One reach each and every person in the world.

NUMATA Yehan
Founder of the English
Tripiṭaka Project

August 7, 1991

Editorial Foreword

In January 1982, Dr. NUMATA Yehan, the founder of the Bukkyō Dendō Kyōkai (Society for the Promotion of Buddhism), decided to begin the monumental task of translating the complete Taishō edition of the Chinese Tripiṭaka (Buddhist canon) into the English language. Under his leadership, a special preparatory committee was organized in April 1982. By July of the same year, the Translation Committee of the English Tripiṭaka was officially convened.

The initial Committee consisted of the following members: (late) HANAYAMA Shōyū (Chairperson), BANDŌ Shōjun, ISHIGAMI Zennō, (late) KAMATA Shigeo, KANAOKA Shūyū, MAYEDA Sengaku, NARA Yasuaki, (late) SAYEKI Shinkō, (late) SHIOIRI Ryōtatsu, TAMARU Noriyoshi, (late) TAMURA Kwansei, URYŪZU Ryūshin, and YUYAMA Akira. Assistant members of the Committee were as follows: KANAZAWA Atsushi, WATANABE Shōgo, Rolf Giebel of New Zealand, and Rudy Smet of Belgium.

After holding planning meetings on a monthly basis, the Committee selected one hundred thirty-nine texts for the First Series of translations, an estimated one hundred printed volumes in all. The texts selected are not necessarily limited to those originally written in India but also include works written or composed in China and Japan. While the publication of the First Series proceeds, the texts for the Second Series will be selected from among the remaining works; this process will continue until all the texts, in Japanese as well as in Chinese, have been published.

Frankly speaking, it will take perhaps one hundred years or more to accomplish the English translation of the complete Chinese and Japanese texts, for they consist of thousands of works. Nevertheless, as Dr. NUMATA wished, it is the sincere hope of the Committee that this project will continue unto completion, even after all its present members have passed away.

It must be mentioned here that the final object of this project is not academic fulfillment but the transmission of the teaching of the

Buddha to the whole world in order to create harmony and peace among humankind. To that end, the translators have been asked to minimize the use of explanatory notes of the kind that are indispensable in academic texts, so that the attention of general readers will not be unduly distracted from the primary text. Also, a glossary of selected terms is appended to aid in understanding the text.

To my great regret, however, Dr. NUMATA passed away on May 5, 1994, at the age of ninety-seven, entrusting his son, Mr. NUMATA Toshihide, with the continuation and completion of the Translation Project. The Committee also lost its able and devoted Chairperson, Professor HANAYAMA Shōyū, on June 16, 1995, at the age of sixty-three. After these severe blows, the Committee elected me, then Vice President of Musashino Women's College, to be the Chair in October 1995. The Committee has renewed its determination to carry out the noble intention of Dr. NUMATA, under the leadership of Mr. NUMATA Toshihide.

The present members of the Committee are MAYEDA Sengaku (Chairperson), ISHIGAMI Zennō, ICHISHIMA Shōshin, KANAOKA Shūyū, NARA Yasuaki, TAMARU Noriyoshi, URYŪZU Ryūshin, YUYAMA Akira, Kenneth K. Tanaka, WATANABE Shōgo, and assistant member YONEZAWA Yoshiyasu.

The Numata Center for Buddhist Translation and Research was established in November 1984, in Berkeley, California, U.S.A., to assist in the publication of the BDK English Tripiṭaka First Series. In December 1991, the Publication Committee was organized at the Numata Center, with Professor Philip Yampolsky as the Chairperson. To our sorrow, Professor Yampolsky passed away in July 1996. In February 1997, Dr. Kenneth K. Inada became Chair and served in that capacity until August 1999. The current Chair, Dr. Francis H. Cook, has been continuing the work since October 1999. All of the remaining texts will be published under the supervision of this Committee, in close cooperation with the Editorial Committee in Tokyo.

MAYEDA Sengaku
Chairperson
Editorial Committee of
the BDK English Tripiṭaka

Publisher's Foreword

The Publication Committee shares with the Editorial Committee the responsibility of realizing the vision of Dr. Yehan Numata, founder of Bukkyō Dendō Kyōkai, the Society for the Promotion of Buddhism. This vision is no less than to make the Buddha's teaching better known throughout the world, through the translation and publication in English of the entire collection of Buddhist texts compiled in the *Taishō Shinshū Daizōkyō,* published in Tokyo in the early part of the twentieth century. This huge task is expected to be carried out by several generations of translators and may take as long as a hundred years to complete. Ultimately, the entire canon will be available to anyone who can read English and who wishes to learn more about the teaching of the Buddha.

The present generation of staff members of the Publication Committee includes Marianne Dresser; Brian Nagata, president of the Numata Center for Buddhist Translation and Research, Berkeley, California; Eisho Nasu; and Reverend Kiyoshi Yamashita. The Publication Committee is headquartered at the Numata Center and, working in close cooperation with the Editorial Committee, is responsible for the usual tasks associated with preparing translations for publication.

In October 1999, I became the third chairperson of the Publication Committee, on the retirement of its very capable former chair, Dr. Kenneth K. Inada. The Committee is devoted to the advancement of the Buddha's teaching through the publication of excellent translations of the thousands of texts that make up the Buddhist canon.

Francis H. Cook
Chairperson
Publication Committee

Contents

THE TREATISE ON THE ELUCIDATION OF THE KNOWABLE

Contents

Translator's Introduction

This text, the *Treatise on the Elucidation of the Knowable* (*Zhangsuozhilun,* Taishō Vol. 32, No. 1645, pp. 226–36), is a Chinese translation from the Tibetan. The *Annals of Buddha and the Patriarchs through the Successive Dynasties (Fozulidaitongzai,* Taishō Vol. 49, No. 2036, pp. 484a–490a), a history of Buddhism in China up to 1333 by Nianchang (1282–1341), also gives a portion of the text, i.e., part I and most of part II, the description of the inanimate and animate worlds. The original Tibetan version was translated into English by Constance Hoog, *Prince Jiṅ-gim's Textbook of Tibetan Buddhism* (Leiden, The Netherlands: E. J. Brill, 1983). A tentative Sanskritization of the title would be *Jñeyaprakāśa-śāstra.* The second and largest of the three parts of the *Čiqula kereglegči,* a Mongolian treatise on Buddhism by Širegetü güüsi čorǰi, written between 1578 and 1607, is based on the Tibetan text and has been studied by Agata Bareja-Starzyńska.

'Phags-pa

The author of this text, the Tibetan 'Phags-pa (1235–1280), whose religious name was Matidhvaja Śrībhadra, was born into a family of abbots and rulers of the Sa-skya Monastery in Tibet, southeast of Lhasa. The ruler of Sa-skya, called Sa-skya Paṇḍita (1182–1251), and his two young nephews, 'Phags-pa and Phyag-na (1239–1267), went to the court of the Mongol ruler in 1247, whose spiritual preceptor Sa-skya became. In 1253 'Phags-pa met the future emperor Qubilai (1215–1294), then still called Sečen, the son of Tolui and grandson of Činggis (ca. 1162–1227). Qubilai ruled from 1260 until his death in 1294. 'Phags-pa became the ruler of Tibet for the Mongols. In 1260 he presided over the enthronement of Qubilai in Qanbaliγ (Beijing) and received the title Guoshi ("National Preceptor"). In 1265 he returned to Sa-skya and remained there until 1268. He then went back to the capital and there devised the quadratic alphabet for Mongolian in 1269. In 1270 he was appointed Dishi ("Imperial Preceptor"), the head of the Buddhist church. In 1275 he again returned to Tibet, accompanied partway by Zhenjin (1243–1285) (Tibetan: Jiṅgim; Mongolian: Čînggim), the crown prince and Qubilai's second son. 'Phags-pa composed for Zhenjin the *Śes-bya rab-gsal* (*Jñeyaprakāśa*), the *Elucidation of the Knowable*. It was finished in Tibet in 1278, delayed by the organization of the religious council in Chu-mig in 1277. Zhenjin's son became Qubilai's successor, Chengzong (r. 1294–1307). 'Phags-pa died in 1280, possibly from poison administered by an attendant.

Śes-rab dpal

Śes-rab dpal (1259–1314), or Shaluoba as he is known in Chinese (religious name Prajñāśrī), was a Xixia, a Tangut monk who was in 'Phags-pa's entourage. He may have known the master 'Phags-pa at the time he was composing this text, a manual for the crown prince Zhenjin, in Tibet. Shaluoba's knowledge of languages served him well as an interpreter for Qubilai. In 1295 he became Inspector General or Overseer of the Buddhist Teaching in all of Jianzhe, and in Fujian in 1298. In 1301 he returned to his native Hexi but went back to the capital in 1308, during the reign of the new emperor Wuzong (r. 1308–1312). During Wuzong's reign Shaluoba received the honorary titles Guanglu Dafu ("Imperial Household Grandee") and Situ ("Grand Instructor").

His successor in the south was another Tangut, dKon-mchog dpal (Ratnaśrī), Guanzhuba in Chinese. From 1302 to 1306 Guanzhuba had the Xixia Tripiṭaka printed in Hangzhou and then distributed in Ningxia and Gansu. He also reinstated the printing of the Jisha edition of the Chinese Tripiṭaka, which had begun during the Song dynasty but was interrupted for a long time.

Shaluoba must have completed the translation of the text before 1306, because it has a postscript by Keji dated November 22, 1306. The colophon does not mention the honorary titles bestowed upon him after his return to Beijing in 1308.

It seems that Shaluoba did the translation work while he was in his native Hexi, probably in 1302. By the way, this is the "mistaken" date given at the end of this text (see note 83). Just as 'Phags-pa had written the text for Zhenjin while in Tibet, having received his knowledge from Sa-skya Paṇḍita, so the Tangut Shaluoba seems to have written his text in Hexi, having received his knowledge from 'Phags-pa. Shaluoba triumphantly returned to Beijing when the new emperor Wuzong began his reign.

Would it be unreasonable to presume that Shaluoba wrote his text with the crown prince in mind during the time of Chengzong? Also, during the reign of Renzong (r. 1312–1320), Shaluoba stayed in the capital, in the Qingshou Monastery, where he died on November 12, 1314. Besides translating this text, Shaluoba is the author of a number of esoteric texts, including the *Yaoshiliuliguangwangqifobenyuangongdejing*, Taishō Nos. 925 and 926; the *Sitātapatra[mahāpratyaṅgirā]dhāraṇī* (*Fodingdabaisangaituoluonijing*), Taishō No. 976, the *Mañjuśrīnāmasaṃgīti* (*Wenshupusazuishengzhenshimingyijing*), Taishō No. 1189; and the *Vajravidāraṇādhāraṇī* (*Huaixiangjingangtuoluonijing*), Taishō No. 1417.

Sources

The second stanza at the end clearly mentions Vasubandhu's *Kośa* (short for *Abhidharmakośa*) as the main source. This is evident throughout the whole work. The *Kośa* was the main doctrinal treatise in Tibet. It is known that there are two Sarvāstivāda scholastic traditions: 1) the Vaibhāṣika "orthodoxy" in Kaśmīra, dominant from the second to seventh centuries, and 2) the Sautrāntikas to the west of Kaśmīra. This was a heterogeneous group of older Sarvāstivādins, called Sautrāntikas since the second century. From the end of the seventh century at least a considerable part of the Sautrāntikas were called Mūlasarvāstivādins. The Abhidharma in China and Japan is Sautrāntika. In Tibet the Abhidharma belongs to the same school of thought (Sautrāntika, Mūlasarvāstivāda).

The central text is Vasubandhu's *Abhidharmakośa* (fifth century). So it is only normal that 'Phags-pa used the *Kośa* to compose his manual. This text does not use the terms Mūlasarvāstivāda or Dārṣṭāntika. It seems these terms had a Vinaya connotation. There hardly are any explicit references to the Vinaya. Sectarian discussions are avoided.

All sources for the text certainly existed in Tibetan versions, a necessity for 'Phags-pa. Texts written by Vasubandhu (ca. 400–480?), the Sautrāntika who became a prominent figure with the Yogācāra school, and by his older brother Asaṅga (born in Gandhāra, ca. 390–470?) certainly were an inspiration to 'Phags-pa. Both brothers are of crucial importance for the study of the Sarvāstivāda (Sautrāntika) school and of Mahayana scholasticism. Very few texts are mentioned by name. The *Abhidharmasamuccaya* (*Dashengepidamojilun*), Taishō Vol. 31, No. 1605, is mentioned. The *Pañcaskandhaka,* on which Vasubandhu wrote a *prakaraṇa,* an explanatory text, is mentioned (see Taishō Vol. 31, No. 1612). This text also quotes from the *Mahāyānasūtrālaṃkāra* (see note 20). Maitreyanātha (ca. 350–430?) may have composed the *kārikā*s (stanzas), and Asaṅga may have written a commentary (*bhāṣya*). Vasubandhu's commentaries on the *Daśabhūmika-sūtra* and the *Pratītyasamutpāda-sūtra* also were a source of inspiration. Another text that was very influential in Tibet was the *Prajñapti-śāstra* (*Lokaprajñapti*). This text seems to have been a source for parts I and II, on the inanimate and animate worlds. Prajñāpāramitā (Perfection of Wisdom) literature also seems to have been a source of inspiration. Definite Mahayana ideas appear at the end of the fourth chapter but no text title is mentioned. Another source seems to have been the *Pañcaviṃśatisāhasrikā*[*prajñāpāramitā-sūtra*] (*Moheboreboluomijing*), Taishō Vol. 8, No. 223. Esoteric terms or ideas do not occur, except perhaps the four wisdoms (see note 66). This is noteworthy in a time when the Tibetan Sa-skya school was so influential. Chan philosophy was still influential in China, but this school was not very important for 'Phags-pa.

This text clearly is acceptable to all Buddhists. At times the explanation is detailed but at other times the text needs a great deal of further explanation—for example, part III, "The Factors of the Path," needs further clarification.

THE TREATISE ON THE ELUCIDATION OF THE KNOWABLE

Composed by

'Phags-pa, Imperial Preceptor of the Yuan

Translated by Śes-rab dpal,
Great Teacher and Propagator of the Buddha's Knowledge,
Tripiṭaka with the Dharma-nature, Overseer of the
Buddhist Teaching, preaching in the regions of the
Yangtze and Huai Rivers and in Fujian

Fascicle One 226b

Homage to my adamantine teacher, and homage to all Buddhas and bodhisattvas.

> 1. In his compassion he has revealed to the beings the contents of his universal knowledge. Homage to his supreme knowledge! I shall elucidate the knowable!
> 2. The inanimate and the animate worlds, the factors of the path and the factors of fruition, and also the unconditioned factors—these are the five topics outlined.

I. The Inanimate World

The substance of the inanimate world consists of the four great elements, because these elements arise simultaneously. Earth is hard. Water is moist. Fire is warm and wind moves. These are the great elements. The smallest parts of these elements are the particles. One might say that they are near-emptinesses, which cannot be fully explained.[1]

Seven of those near-emptinesses are one particle. Seven of those particles are an atom. Seven of those atoms are a gold atom. Seven of those gold atoms are a water atom. Seven of those water atoms are [the width of the tip of] a hare's hair. Seven of those hare's hairs are a sheep's hair. Seven of those sheep's hairs are a bullock's hair. Seven of those bullock's hairs are [a dust mote seen in] a fissure. Seven of those fissures are the size of a nit. Seven of those nit-sizes are the size of a louse. Seven of those louses are the size of a barleycorn. Seven of those barleycorn-sizes are a finger-joint. Three joints are one inch. A spread of twenty-four inches is one cubit. Four cubits are one arc. Five hundred arcs make one *krośa*. Eight *krośa*s make one *yojana*. These are the measurements for the shapes in the world.

As for the cause that establishes the world, it comes from the influence of the common deeds of all sentient beings. How is it established? From the sphere of empty space arise winds from the ten directions. Rushing at each other, they become firm and motionless, forming the circle of subtle wind.[2] Its color is light blue and it is extremely solid. It is sixteen *lakṣas*[3] of *yojana*s deep and its extent is immeasurable. From its heat comes a cloud, called Suvarṇagarbha ("Golden Repository"). It brings a heavy downpour of rain and it is supported by the wind. This is namely the ocean below, which is eleven *lakṣa*s and twenty thousand *yojana*s deep and twelve *lakṣa*s and three thousand four hundred and fifty *yojana*s wide. As that water is stirred [by the wind] it curdles on
226c top and becomes gold, just as when one cooks milk it coagulates on top and forms a skin. Because of the circle of the golden earth, the circle of water decreases to just eight *lakṣa*s (*yojana*s) thick. The remainder is formed little by little and the gold becomes three *lakṣa*s and twenty thousand *yojana*s thick. The circle of gold and the circle of water are equally wide. Their circumference is three times as big, thirty-six *lakṣa*s and ten thousand three hundred and fifty *yojana*s on the whole.

The previous circle of wind is the ground for the Sahā world. The two circles of earth and water are the ground of the world of the four [great] continents. On top of the circle of earth further heavy rains fall. They form the great ocean, stirred by the wind. A mass of the finest quality forms Mount Sumeru. A mass of intermediate quality forms the Seven Golden Mountains. A mass of the lowest quality forms Mount Cakravāḍa. A mass of mixed quality forms the four continents. As for the substances of [Mount] Sumeru, in the east it is made of silver (*rūpya*), in the south of beryl (*vaiḍūrya*), in the west of crystal (*sphaṭika*), and in the north of gold (*suvarṇa*). The other seven are gold only. The four continents are made of a mixture of elements, [such as] earth and so on. Mount Cakravāḍa is made only of iron.

As to its size, Mount Sumeru is submerged eighty thousand *yojana*s in the water. Being higher and finer than all other mountains, it is called Sumeru. Then successively [there are] the Seven Golden Mountains: 1) Mount Yugaṃdhara, which is forty thousand *yojana*s high; 2) Mount Īśādhara, which is twenty thousand *yojana*s high; 3) Mount Khadiraka, which is ten thousand *yojana*s high; 4) Mount Sudarśana, which is five thousand *yojana*s high; 5) Mount Aśvakarṇa, which is two thousand five hundred *yojana*s high; 6) Mount Vinataka, which is one thousand two hundred and fifty *yojana*s high; 7) Mount Nimiṃdhara, which is six hundred and twenty-five *yojana*s high. (The commentary of the Tibetan treatise has: 1] Mount Yoke Holder, 2] Mount Ploughbeam Holder, 3] Mount Acacia, 4] Mount Good-looking, 5] Mount Horse's Ear, 6] Mount Elephant's Tusk, 7] Mount Fish Mouth.) Beyond the four great continents is Mount Cakravāḍa, which is three hundred and twelve and a half *yojana*s high. Their width for each of those is equal to their height above the water. Between the Seven Golden Mountains is the place where the dragon (*nāga*) kings amuse themselves, called Lalitasāgara.

Between the eight mountains there are seven oceans. The one nearest to Mount Sumeru is 1) the Yugaṃdhara Ocean, eighty thousand *yojana*s wide. Then there is 2) the Īśādhara Ocean, forty thousand *yojana*s wide; 3) the Khadiraka Ocean, twenty thousand *yojana*s wide; 4) the Sudarśana Ocean, ten thousand *yojana*s wide; 5) the Aśvakarṇa Ocean, five thousand *yojana*s wide; 6) the Vinataka Ocean, two thousand five hundred *yojana*s wide; and 7) the Nimiṃdhara Ocean, one thousand two hundred fifty *yojana*s wide. They are full of water possessing the eight qualities.[4]

The appearance of the eight mountains and the seven oceans is that all lie in a square. The outer ocean tastes salty. The distance between the two mountains Nimiṃdhara and Cakravāḍa is three *lakṣa*s and twenty-two thousand *yojana*s.

Although there are no divisions in the waters of the outer ocean, because of the color of [Mount] Sumeru the color of the ocean in the east is white. The color of the ocean in the south is bluish green. The color of the ocean in the west is red. The color of the ocean in the north is yellow. As they manifest these colors they

227a are called the four seas. Its perimeter is thirty-six *lakṣa*s and seven hundred and fifty *yojana*s. The circumference of the outer Mount Cakravāḍa is thirty-six *lakṣa*s and two thousand six hundred and twenty-five *yojana*s.

In the south of the outer ocean is the continent Jambu[dvīpa]. Its shape is like a chariot. It is narrow toward [Mount] Cakravāḍa, three and a half *yojana*s. The remaining three sides are each two thousand *yojana*s. Its circumference is six thousand three and a half *yojana*s. It has two intermediate continents: in the east Cāmara ("Yak") and in the west Aparacāmara ("Superior Yak"). The center of Jambu[dvīpa] is the land of Magadha, the place where the Buddhas of the three periods come into existence. Then, to the north, beyond nine black mountains, is the great snowy mountain [Himavat], said to possess auspiciousness (Śrīmat). North of that mountain there is Mount Gandhamādana.[5] Between these two mountains there is a great dragon king, called Anavatapta. The lake in which he dwells is called Anavatapta ("Without Heat").[6] Its shape is square, each side fifty *yojana*s. Its circumference is two hundred *yojana*s. The lake is filled with water possessing the eight qualities.

From this lake come the four great rivers. In the east the Ganges River. It flows forth with silver sand from [a rock like] an elephant's mouth. Together with five hundred rivers it flows to the Eastern Ocean. In the south the Indus River. It flows forth with beryl sand from [a rock like] a bull's mouth. Together with five hundred rivers it flows to the Southern Ocean. In the west the Oxus (Vakṣu) River. It flows forth with crystal sand from [a rock like] a horse's mouth. Together with five hundred rivers it flows to the Western Ocean. In the north the Śītā River.[7] It flows forth with gold sand from [a rock like] a lion's mouth. Together with five hundred rivers it flows to the Northern Ocean. These four rivers go around Lake Anavatapta seven times, keeping it to the right, and then flow in their own direction.

Twenty *yojana*s to the north beyond Mount Gandhamādana there is a cliff called the Golden Prāgbhāra Cliff.[8] Each side being fifty *yojana*s, the circumference is two hundred *yojana*s. It is three and a half *yojana*s high. There are eight thousand more smaller cliffs.

Twenty *yojana*s to the north beyond the cliff is the king of the *śāla* trees, called Supratiṣṭhita. Its roots go down forty arcs into the ground and it is eighty arcs high. Seven rows of trees surround it. Twenty *yojana*s to the east beyond it, there is Lake Mandākinī. Its shape is round, fifty *yojana*s wide, and it has a circumference of a hundred and fifty *yojana*s. It further has eighty thousand smaller lakes, and is filled with water possessing the eight qualities. In it there are lotus flowers, of which the leaves are like ox-hide. Their stalks are like axle trees and their flowers are like wagon wheels. Their flavor is fine, just like honey. In that place (Golden Cliff), together with eight thousand elephants, there [is] the elephant king Supratiṣṭhita, who is ridden by Lord Śakra when he goes into battle. He spends the four winter months on the Golden Cliff. He spends the four months of the hot season near the Supratiṣṭhita [tree]. He spends the four rainy months near Lake Mandākinī.

On the shore of Lake Anavatapta there is a *jambu* tree. Its fruits taste fine and have the measurements of a jar. When they are ripe they fall into the water and make the sound *jambu*. The 227b
dragons (*nāga*s) change into fishes and swallow this fruit. [The fruits that are] left over are taken by the current and form *jambu* gold. Because of the name of this tree, (this continent) is called Jambu[dvīpa].

To the west of this continent is the great Adamantine Palace of the land of Oḍḍiyāna,[9] where those of noble lineage dwell. The law of the Adamantine Vehicle (Vajrayana) is transmitted from there. A mountain in the Southern Ocean is called Potalaka. The bodhisattva Avalokiteśvara dwells on its top, and the noble mother Tārā dwells at its foot. In the east there are the Five Peaks (Wutaishan). The bodhisattva Mañjuśrī dwells at the top. There are sixteen great countries and one thousand or so smaller countries. There further are three hundred and sixty different peoples and seven hundred and twenty different languages.

The continent to the east of the outer ocean is called Videha, which is shaped like a half-moon. The side opposite Mount Sumeru is three hundred and fifty *yojanas*. The other side is six thousand *yojanas*. Its circumference is six thousand three hundred and fifty *yojanas*. This continent has two intermediate continents at its two sides: Deha ("Body") to the north and Videha ("Excellent Body") to the south. Those three continents surpass the other continents with seven *tāla* trees. Some say, "The appearance of the people of the continent is fine. Because their person is excellent, it is called Videha."

The northern continent of the outer ocean is called Kuru. Its shape is four-cornered, like a square, each side [measuring] two thousand *yojanas*. Its circumference is eight thousand *yojanas*. This continent has two intermediate continents at its two sides. One is called Kurava ("With Excellence") and the other Kaurava ("Relating to Kurava"). Everything that is enjoyed by the people of that continent comes from the wishing tree. Seven days before their death an unpleasant voice comes from the wishing tree, saying, "In seven days you will die." Some say, "The lowly tongue of the people of the continent is cut. Therefore Kuru means 'unpleasant voice' in the language of the flesh-eating demons (*piśācas*)."

The western continent of the outer ocean is called Godānīya. Its shape is like the full moon. Its diameter is two thousand five hundred *yojanas* and its circumference is seven thousand five hundred *yojanas*. It has two intermediate continents: to the south Śāṭhā ("With Deceit") and to the north Uttaramantriṇa ("Supreme Deportment"). Because the people in that continent possess a great many precious cows, it is called Godānīya.

The continents, oceans, and mountains are on the underside all eighty thousand *yojanas*, because they are near the Golden Ground. The continents Siṃhala[dvīpa], Suvarṇadvīpa, Candradvīpa,[10] and so on, near Jambudvīpa, belong to Jambudvīpa. The same applies to the small continents of the other great continents.

Upward from there, forty thousand *yojanas* in space, on the circle of wind which is pure, unobstructed, and very firm, are the sun, moon, and stars, moving around from the right. The gods who dwell in space dwell and abide there.

The disc of the sun is made of a fire crystal. Its diameter is fifty-one *yojana*s and its circumference a hundred and fifty-three *yojana*s. It is six and one-eighteenth *yojana*s thick. On top it has a golden rim. Higher up there further are gold, silver, beryl, and crystal, which delicately form four spires. It is the palace where the Sun God and his retinue dwell. It is put into motion by the 227c
wind and it goes round the four great continents in one day and night. When the sun goes north, the day becomes longer. When it goes south, the time becomes shorter. When it goes between north and south, [the length of the] day and night are equal. Because of the light in the places where it proceeds there is cold and heat, and it brings the time of winter and summer. It goes six months to the north and six months to the south. When it has reached halfway, this is called the turning back of the sun and moon. Going once round the circle of the stars is called one year.

The disc of the moon is made of water crystal. Its diameter is fifty *yojana*s and its circumference is one hundred and fifty *yojana*s. It is six and one-eighteenth *yojana*s thick. On top there further are gold, silver, beryl, and crystal, which delicately form four spires. It is the palace where the Moon God and his retinue dwell. As the distance between the sun and the moon is far or near, its own shadow increases and diminishes. As it increases one part, the waxing moon emerges. When the fifteen parts are complete, it is called full. As it diminishes one part, the waning moon emerges. When its own shadow covers it and when the fifteen parts are complete, it is called not full. Because of the increase or decrease one uses the term sky-day. Because of one day and one night, one uses the term earth-day. Such thirty [of these days] are called one month.

The stars are the palaces of the gods who dwell in space. They are made of precious materials and their shape is in any case round. The smallest is one *krośa*, the middle size is three *krośa*s, and the biggest is six *krośa*s. Their circumference is threefold, belonging to the group of the [Four Great Heavenly Kings] (*caturmahārājaka-kāyika*).

On Mount Sumeru there are four terraces. The one of which the distance from the water level upward is ten times one thousand *yojanas* is the first terrace. From Mount Sumeru's sides it protrudes sixteen times one thousand *yojanas*. The one which is ten thousand *yojanas* upward is the second terrace. It protrudes eight thousand *yojanas* from the sides. The one which is ten thousand *yojanas* upward is the third terrace. It protrudes four thousand *yojanas* from the sides. The one which is ten thousand *yojanas* upward is the fourth terrace, which protrudes two thousand *yojanas* from the sides. The four corners at the top of that Mount Sumeru each have a pinnacle that is four and a half *yojanas* high, one hundred and twenty-five *yojanas* wide, and five hundred *yojanas* in circumference. There are *yakṣa* spirits living there.

On top of the mountain is the central city of the thirty-three gods (Trāyastriṃśa), called Sudarśana, which is made from pure gold. It is one and a half *yojanas* high, with each side two thousand five hundred *yojanas*, and ten thousand *yojanas* in circumference. Its walls are pure gold, all adorned with one hundred and one different precious gems. The earth is soft like *tūla* cotton. On the four sides of that city there are sixteen thousand precious pillars, and there are precious ridges, precious rafters, and precious eaves. [There are] four gates at the four sides, and further one thousand minus one smaller gates. [There are] four main thoroughfares, with smaller streets. By the four gates are five hundred gods guarding those gates, all wearing solid armor.

In the city there is the palace of Emperor Śakra, called Vaijayanta ("Most Excellent Abode" or "Very Excellent Palace"). Its shape is square. It is four and a half *yojanas*[11] high, and each of
228a the sides is two hundred and fifty *yojanas*. Its circumference is one thousand *yojanas*. [There are] one hundred and one domes (*niryūhas*) and for each dome there are seven pavilions. For each precious pavilion [there are] seven smaller pavilions, and for each smaller pavilion [there are] seven ponds. For each pond [there are] seven lotuses, and on each lotus there are seven boys and girls, playing different kinds of music, singing, dancing, and being merry.

To the east of the city of Sudarśana there is [the place] where all ride, called Caitraratha Park, on an elevation of one thousand *yojanas*. To the south is the place for those who go into battle, called Pāruṣyaka Park. To the west [is] the place for all [kinds of] behavior, called Miśraka Park. To the north [is] the place for merriment, called Nandana Park. Their extent is the same as the first one.

At a distance of twenty *yojanas* beyond these parks there are beautiful grounds, called Caitraratha, Pāruṣyaka, Miśraka, and Nandana, of the same size as the four parks. To the northeast of Sudarśana there is the wishing tree, called Pārijātaka, also called the "fully-developed" tree. Its roots go down fifty *yojanas*, and it is one hundred *yojanas* high. Its branches extend over fifty *yojanas*. It grants one's wishes. Under it is a stone slab, called Armolika, [which is] as white as a cloth (*pāṇḍukambalaśilātala*). [Measuring] fifty *yojanas* on each side, its circumference is two hundred *yojanas*. To the southwest of Sudarśana is the place where the gods gather, called the Sudharmā Hall. Its circumference is nine hundred *yojanas* and its shape is round. In the middle of that hall is the throne of Emperor Śakra, made of pure gold. Around this throne are the seats of the thirty-two assisting officials. In all [the seats of] the thirty-three gods are arranged.

Eighty thousand *yojanas* upward is the palace of the Yāma gods, made from precious materials and resting on the wind in space. Its size is twice as big as the top of Mount Sumeru. One hundred and sixty thousand *yojanas* higher is the palace of the Tuṣita gods, made from valuables and resting on the wind in space. Its measurements are like those of the Yāma [heaven], but the extent is twice as big. Three *lakṣas* and twenty thousand *yojanas* higher is the palace of the Nirmāṇarati gods, made from valuables and resting on the wind in space. Its measurements are like those of the Tuṣita [heaven], but the extent is twice as big. Six *lakṣas* and forty thousand *yojanas* higher is the palace of the Paranirmitavaśavartin gods, made from valuables and resting on the wind in space. Its measurements are the same as those of the Nirmāṇarati [heaven], but the extent is twice as big. This is the realm of desire (*kāmadhātu*). Above it is the first meditative trance (*dhyāna*). And so the four [great] continents, the seven mountains, Mount Sumeru and Mount Cakravāḍa, the six gods of the realm of desire, and the first trance are the so-called realm of the four continents.

Up to a thousand are a small chiliocosm. One small chiliocosm is surrounded by a Mount Cakravāḍa. Up to a thousand of these small chiliocosms are a medium chiliocosm. One medium chiliocosm is surrounded by a Mount Cakravāḍa. Up to a thousand of these medium chiliocosms are a trichiliocosm. One trichiliocosm is surrounded by a Mount Cakravāḍa. And so there are a hundred times one hundred thousand realms of the four continents, all
228b spread out surrounded by Mount Cakravāḍas.

In the dark places between the mountains of the continents there is no day or night. When you raise your hand you see nothing. The heaven of the first trance is equal in size to the realm of the four continents. The heaven of the second trance is equal in size to a small chiliocosm. The heaven of the third trance is equal in size to a medium chiliocosm. The heaven of the fourth trance is equal in size to a trichiliocosm. The distance between them always increases twofold. This is namely the realm of form (*rūpadhātu*).

The realm of non-form (*ārūpyadhātu*) has no separate places. If someone is born there, he is [re]born in the place where his life had ended. Because one dwells in an immaterial meditative attainment, it is called the [realm of] non-form.

II. The Animate World

The animate world is altogether sixfold: 1) hell[-beings], 2) hungry ghosts (*preta*s), 3) animals, 4) humans, 5) *asura*s, and 6) gods (*deva*s). What do the names of these six kinds mean? First, because [their limbs are] cut to pieces, they are called hell-beings. Second, as they are vexed by hunger and thirst, they are called hungry ghosts. Third, because they walk horizontally, they are called animals. Fourth, because their mind makes many distinctions, they are called humans, the meaning of *manuṣya*. Fifth, because even though their bodies and enjoyments are like those of the gods, they are somewhat inferior, or because of the absence of wine (*surā*), they are called demigods, the meaning of *asura*. Sixth, because they are born of a Brahma body and are merry and joyful, or because they are worthy of worship, they are called gods, the meaning of *deva*.

Hell is a wasteland twenty thousand *yojana*s under the Jambu[dvīpa] continent. Its four sides are twenty thousand *yojana*s. It is made entirely of iron, and is thoroughly incandescent with fire. There are eight hot hells: 1) Saṃjīva, 2) Kālasūtra, 3) Saṃghāta, 4) Raurava, 5) Mahāraurava, 6) Tāpana, 7) Pratāpana, and 8) Avīci.[12]

As for the Saṃjīva hell, the beings who are born there are affected by their former deeds. Holding weapons in their hands they harbor enmity toward one another and cut each other down. They fall to pieces, faint, and temporarily die. When a voice from space revives them, these beings are immediately revived and they again cut each other down. As for their lifespan, the period of one life of the gods of the Four Great Heavenly Kings is one day and night. Their lifetime, thus calculated, is five hundred years of experiencing this suffering.

As for the Kālasūtra hell, the hell guards mark the bodies of the beings from head to toe with black threads and cleave their limbs with flaming saws and axes. Through the power of their former deeds the upper part [of the body] revives when they have cut away the lower part. As for their lifespans, the period of one life of the Trāyastriṃśa gods is one day and night. Their lifetime, thus calculated, is one thousand years of experiencing this suffering.

As for the Saṃghāta hell, the beings who are born there are hit with iron hammers. Or there are two iron mountains, like a ram's head. When the two mountains come together, [the beings] are ground down and crushed. When the two mountains open up, they are spontaneously revived and are crushed again. As for their lifespans, the period of one life of the Yāma gods is one day and

228c night. Their lifetime, thus calculated, is two thousand years of experiencing this suffering.

As for the Raurava hell, the beings who are born there are frightened by a pool of hot iron. As they enter a dense forest it is ablaze with flames and they burn [for] long years. Because of the power of their former deeds the extent of their tongue measures one thousand *yojana*s. There is a big ox with iron horns and hooves and equipped with an iron plough. Ablaze with flames, it ploughs their tongues. As for their lifespans, the period of one life of the Tuṣita gods is one day and night. Their lifetime, thus calculated, is four thousand years of experiencing this suffering.

As for the Mahāraurava hell, it is the same as the previous one, but [the] suffering [experienced by those reborn there] is twice as great. As for their lifespans, the period of one life of the Nirmāṇarati gods is one day and night. Their lifetime, thus calculated, is eight thousand years of experiencing this suffering.

As for the Tāpana hell, [the beings born there] experience suffering within three iron walls and are utterly destroyed by fire. As for their lifespans, the period of one life of the Paranirmitavaśavartin gods is one day and night. The length of such life is sixteen thousand years of experiencing this suffering.

As for the Pratāpana hell, it is the same as the previous one, but [the] suffering [experienced by those who are reborn there] is twice as great. Their lifetime equals half an intermediate *kalpa* (*antarakalpa*)[13] of experiencing this suffering.

In the Avīci hell [beings] experience extreme suffering. Their bodies are ablaze in flames in an iron room. Their lifetime equals one intermediate *kalpa*.

As for the sixteen supplementary hells, alongside the eight hot hells there are four on each side.[14] They are: the [first] supplementary hell, Kukkula, in which all sink up to their knees. When beings go there, the moment they put down their foot their skin, flesh, and blood are all burned and fall off, leaving only bones. When they lift their feet, they grow again, restored as before.

The [second] supplementary hell is Kuṇapa, in which beings

sink up to their waist in impurity and filth full of many *nyaṅkuṭā* insects, whose snouts are as sharp as needles. They pierce the skin to the bone and suck out the marrow.

The [third] supplementary hell is Kṣuradhārā, further threefold: 1) Kṣuramārga—[sharp] blades are spread out there, forming a large path. When beings go there, the moment they put down a foot, their skin, flesh, and blood are all cut up and fall off. When they lift their feet, they grow again, restored as before; 2) Asipattravana—the trees in this forest have sharp swords as leaves. When beings go there, the wind blows down the leaves, cutting up their limbs. Their flesh and bones fall down. There are fierce black dogs that pull at them with their fangs and eat them; and 3) the forest with the iron thorns, called [Ayaḥ]śālmalī[vana]—the trees in this forest have sharp iron thorns, sixteen inches long. When beings are forced up and down the trees, the sharp edges of the thorns stab them up and down. The blood, flesh, and skin of these beings hang on the thorns and stain them, leaving only sinews and the bones. There are ravens with an iron beak that peck at the eyes and at the brain of the beings, contending to eat them. These three kinds, Kṣuramārga, and so on, may be different but because the iron weapons are the same, they are comprised in one supplementary hell [called Kṣuradhārā].

The [fourth] supplementary hell Kṣārodakā Nadī, called 229a
Vaitaraṇī ("Without Ford"), is filled with an extremely potent alkaline fluid. When a being enters it, he may drift or sink, go against or with the flow, go sideways or vertically. He is cooked and boiled and his flesh and bones disintegrate. If, for example, one were to place grains of rice in a big cauldron filled with lye and burn a fierce fire under it, the grains of rice in it would go up and down and around and completely decompose. The same applies to [the] beings [reborn in this hell]. If they try to escape, there are guards on both shores, who hold knives and spears in their hands, keeping them off [the shore] and forcing them to return. There is no way they can escape. This river is like a moat and the previous three are like parks. They are called nearby hells.

[There are] eight cold hells: 1) Arbuda, 2) Nirarbuda, 3) Aṭaṭa, 4) Apapa (Hahava), 5) Huhuva, 6) Bursting Open Like an Utpala Flower (i.e., a blue lotus), 7) Bursting Open Like a Red Lotus (*padma*), and 8) Bursting Open Like a Very Red Lotus (*mahā-padma*).[15]

In the Arbuda hell, [beings are] born in frozen ice; there is extremely severe cold and they have blisters all over, which is the meaning of Arbuda hell. As for their lifespan, if you take one sesame [seed] every hundred years from eighty bushels of sesame [seeds]—the large bushels used in the land of Magadha—until the sesame [seeds] are used up, their lifetime [in this hell] is just like that.

In the Nirarbuda hell, because of extremely severe cold the blisters burst open and yellow pus drips out. The lifespan [of the beings born there] is twenty times longer than in the preceding hell.

In the Aṭaṭa hell, because of very severe cold the [beings born there] bear it with shattering teeth. Their lifespan is twenty times longer than in the preceding [hell].

In the Apapa hell, [the beings born there] wail while enduring the cold. Their lifespan is twenty times longer than in the preceding [hell].

In the Huhuva hell, [the beings born there] emit a painful sound because they cry from cold. Their lifespan is twenty times longer than in the preceding [hell].

In the hell Bursting Open Like an Utpala Flower, because of the severe cold the body bursts open like the leaves of an *utpala* flower. The lifespan [of the beings born there] is twenty times longer than in the preceding [hell].

In the hell Bursting Open Like a Red Lotus, because of the severe cold the body bursts open, opening up like a red lotus. The lifespan [of the beings born there] is twenty times longer than in the preceding [hell].

In the hell Bursting Open Like a Very Red Lotus, the body bursts open even worse than in the preceding [hell], just as a big red lotus opens up its many leaves. The lifespan [of the beings born there] is twenty times longer than in the preceding [hell].

The individual hells are in the wilderness and the mountains of Jambudvīpa. Each day and night one experiences [both] suffering and happiness, because the feelings are mixed together. And so the eight hot hells, the eight cold hells, the supplementary hells, and the individual hells are called the eighteen hells.

In the second place,[16] the hungry ghosts. Five hundred *yojana*s under the city of Rājagṛha there is the city of the hungry ghosts, called Kapila ("Yellowish White"), also called Candan ("Somber"). The demon king is called Dharma King Yama. He dwells together with thirty-six attendants.

There are four kinds [of hungry ghosts]: 1) those with an outer obstacle, 2) those with an inner obstacle, 3) those with an obstacle to food and drink, and 4) those with an obstacle to eating and drinking. First are those with an outer obstacle—they cannot even hear the sound of eating and drinking. Second, those with an inner obstacle may obtain some food and drink but it cannot get in, as their 229b
mouth is like the eye of a needle. Supposing [the food] can enter the mouth, the throat is like a horse's tail (i.e., as narrow as a horse hair). [The food] cannot pass through. [Even] supposing [the food] passes through the throat, the belly, having the dimensions of a mountain, can never be filled. Even if the belly is filled, their legs are like the stalk of a plant and cannot lift it. They experience this great suffering. Third are those with an obstacle to food and drink. When they see food and drink, countless guards take up arms and guard it, not letting anyone obtain it. Fourth are those with an obstacle to eating and drinking. When they take food and drink, affected by their deeds, iron balls and liquid bronze are put in their mouths and flow straight out from below. Such four kinds are all hungry ghosts. As for their lifespans, one month among people equals one night and day. In this way one calculates their lifetimes to be five hundred years, which equals fifteen thousand human years. Some stay among humans, in such places as cemeteries, eating flesh and blood. These all are the kinds of hungry ghosts.

In the third place are the animals. They mostly live in rivers and seas, and dwell in turbid waters like dregs. Since the big ones eat the small ones and the small ones eat the big ones, they all fear one another. Because of the waves of the sea, their dwelling places are not fixed. Some dwell among humans and gods. As for their lifespans, the longest is like the life of a dragon (*nāga*) king, half an intermediate *kalpa*, and the shortest is like the life of a gnat, that is, one instant (*kṣaṇa*). The size of their bodies is not fixed.

In the fourth place are humans. They live in the four great continents, in the eight intermediate continents, and in the minor continents. As for their lifespans, for example the lifetime of the people of Jambudvīpa was immeasurable in the initial origination *kalpa*. Thereafter it gradually decreased to sixty years now, and it will continue to gradually decrease to ten years. After that it may gradually increase but without any fixed duration. The people of Kuru to the north definitely live one thousand years. The people of Videha to the east live five hundred years. The people of Godānīya to the west live two hundred and fifty years. Except for those of Kuru to the north, the others may meet an untimely end.

As for their objects of enjoyment, those of the continent Kuru to the north consume natural wild rice. Their clothes and necklaces come from the wishing tree. Those of the other three continents consume cereals and meat, and they have the enjoyment of riches and valuables.

As for the size of their bodies, the people of Jambudvīpa [measure four cubits and the people of Videha to the east[17]] measure eight cubits. The [size of the bodies] of the people of Godānīya to the west is sixteen cubits. The people of Kuru to the north are thirty-two cubits [in size]. The face of those people is like the shape of their continent. The people of the smaller continents are like those of the main continents but in each case their bodies have decreased to half [their size]. So they are explained in this way.

In the fifth place are the *asura*s (demigods). Eleven thousand *yojana*s under the level of the waters of Mount Sumeru, in the city of Sāṃkāśya in a mountainous wasteland, lives the *asura* king called Rāhu ("Composing the Mind") with his retinue. Eleven thousand *yojana*s farther lives the *asura* king called Śambara (?) ("Neck

Garland") with his retinue in the city of Tārāmālā (?) ("Star Garland"). Eleven thousand *yojanas* farther lives the *asura* king called Prahārāda (?) ("Fine Guardian") or Bali ("Strong") with his retinue in the city of Dṛḍha (?) ("Stronghold"). Eleven thousand 229c
yojanas farther lives the *asura* king called Vemacitra ("Variety of Strings" or "Multitude of Decorative Lines") with his retinue in the city of Gambhīra ("Deep"). He is in a constant battle with his opponent Lord Śakra. His fortress is called Haimavatī ("Golden") and his palace is called Ninādita (?) ("Music"). His wishing tree king is called Citrapāṭalī. His meeting place is called Sudhana and his stone slab is called Bhadra. His parks are called Joy, Fine Joy, Utmost Joy, and Entire Joy, and his fine grounds are also called Joy, Fine Joy, Utmost Joy, and Entire Joy. The elephant he rides into battle is called Duṣprasāha. The elephant he rides to enjoy himself is called Snowdrift, and his horse is called Balāhaka.

The *asuras* fight with the thirty-three gods (Trāyastriṃśa) over the flavor of *sudhā* (divine nectar) and the *asura* lady [Śacī]. They come out of the mountainous wasteland in order to wage battle. Wearing solid armor made of gold, silver, beryl, or crystal, and wielding swords, spears, javelins, or bows and arrows, they lead their four divisions. Either the first three of the *asura* kings, Rāhu, Śambara, and Prahārāda, come or all four, including Vemacitra, come. At that time, of the five groups of protectors of Lord Śakra, the one dwelling in the Lalitasāgara, the group of the dragon (*nāga*) kings who rejoice in white (i.e, wholesome) factors wage battle against the *asura* armies in order to drive them back. If the *nāgas* are not victorious, they go to the Karoṭapāṇi [gods] and the two protectors again both wage battle against the *asuras*. If they are still not victorious, they further go to the Mālādhāra [gods] and all three protectors again wage battle against the *asuras*. If they are not victorious, they further go to the Sadāmata [gods] and all four protectors again wage battle against the *asuras*. If they are still not victorious, they further go to the Four [Great Heavenly] Kings and all five protectors again wage battle against the *asuras*. The Four Great

Heavenly Kings lead their four armies, donning their precious solid armor and grasping their weapons.

The Four [Great] Heavenly Kings usually win in battle, but if they cannot hold them back, they go to the Trāyastriṃśa gods and inform Lord Śakra, "We, the protectors, cannot drive the *asura* armies back. You, king, must rout the enemy!" When they have thus spoken, Lord Śakra, lord of the gods, mounts his elephant Supratiṣṭhita and informs the group of the thirty-three gods: "You must know that the *asura* armies have now reached the top of Mount Sumeru! Don your solid armor and take your chariots to fight against the *asura*s!" After he has said these words, the divine sons all don their precious armor and grasp their weapons. They go to Caitraratha Park and take their chariots and, entering Pāruṣyaka Park, they steel their bodies and minds. Upon leaving the city of Sudarśana, they engage the battle with their enemies, the *asura*s.

If the *asura*s are victorious, they invade the city. If the gods gain a victory, they pursue the chariots of the *asura*s to the first sea. If the gods or *asura*s are cut at the waist in a battle they die, but if their hands and feet are cut off, the [limbs] regrow again, just as before. When a Bhagavat, a *pratyekabuddha,* or a noble universal monarch (*cakravartin*) dwells in the world, the *asura*s do not have any belligerent thoughts, but if they come to blows, the gods will certainly be victorious. If that which is wholesome
230a in the world increases, the multitude of the gods will also win. If that which is not wholesome in the world increases, the *asura*s will win; thus, the gods protect wholesome elements.

In the sixth place are the gods.[18] [There are] six gods in the realm of desire, seventeen in the realm of form, and four in the realm of non-form. Of the six gods of the realm of desire, on the first terrace of Mount Sumeru the group of Karoṭapāṇi [gods] lives. On the second terrace the group of Mālādhāra [gods] lives. On the third terrace the group of Sadāmada [gods] lives. To the north on Mount Yugaṃdhara there is a fortress called Aṭakāvatī, the dwelling of the heavenly king Vaiśravaṇa and his multitude of *yakṣa*s. In the same way, to the east there is a fortress called Excellent, where the great heavenly king Dhṛtarāṣṭra and his multitude of *gandharvas* live. To the west there is a fortress called Various Forms, where the great heavenly king Virūpākṣa and his multitude of *nāga* spirits live. To the south there is a fortress called Virūḍhaka, where the great heavenly king Virūḍhaka and his multitude of *yamāntakas* (*kumbhāṇḍas*) live. For the rest, on the four terraces, the Seven Golden Mountains, the sun, moon, and stars, Mount Cakravāḍa, in the mountains of the Jambu[dvīpa] continent, in the *tāla* trees, a multitude belonging to the group of the Four [Great Heavenly] Kings also dwell in [these] places. They all form the company of the Four [Great Heavenly] Kings. They are namely one group. As for their lifespan, fifty human years are one night and day. In this way their lifetime measures five hundred years. As for the size of their bodies, it is one-fourth of a *krośa*.

On top of Mount Sumeru with the thirty-three gods dwells Lord Śakra, lord of the gods, in the place Vaijayanta, together with his *asura* lady called Śacī, and also with many goddesses (*apsaras*). They tirelessly enjoy their desires. There is also the royal elephant that [Śakra] rides into battle, called Supratiṣṭhita. The royal elephant he rides in his park for amusement is called Airāvaṇa ("Offspring Possessing the Earth"). These two elephants each have a girth of seven *yojanas*, and each lives with a group of eight thousand smaller elephants. There also is a royal horse called Balāhaka, which dwells with eight thousand horses. Because the number of the assisting officials of the lord of the gods is thirty-two,[19] they are [collectively] called the thirty-three gods.

All heavenly sons indulge in the five desires. When they are heedless, there is a big celestial drum (*mahābheri*) and the tones that come from the drum arouse the gods. They say, "All formations are impermanent, impure, and all are painful. All factors are egoless. Their allayment means happiness."[20] When they fight with the *asura* armies, it brings tones that dispel suffering, arousing them with the words, "The gods wish to obtain a victory, and they wish for the defeat of the *asuras*." The palace, the fortress, the tree, the meeting places, the stone [slab], and so on are as discussed earlier.[21]

As for the lifespan of the gods, a hundred human years are one night and day. Calculated in this way, their lifetime is a thousand years. Their celestial bodies measure half a *yojana*.

The Yāma gods: the thirty-three gods fight with the *asura*s, but because [the Yāma gods] are free from strife, they are called gods who are free from strife (Yāma). As for the lifespan of these gods, two hundred years are one night and day. Calculated in this way their lifetime is two thousand years. Their celestial bodies measure two *yojana*s.

230b The Tuṣita gods: there is the venerable Maitreya who will succeed to the throne of the Dharma King, both mundane and supramundane. Experiencing the happiness of the great doctrine, they are called Tuṣita. This means "all happy." Four hundred years among humans are one night and day of those gods. Their lifetime is four thousand years and their bodies measure four *yojana*s.

The Nirmāṇarati gods: enjoying their own magical creations, they are called Nirmāṇarati. Eight hundred years among humans are one night and day of those gods. Their lifetime is eight thousand years and their bodies measure eight *yojana*s.

The Paranirmitavaśavartin gods: enjoying the magical creations of others, they are called Paranirmitavaśavartin. The celestial king among them, their awesome sovereign, is Lord Māra. One thousand six hundred years among humans are one night and day of those gods. Their lifetime measures sixteen thousand years and their bodies measure sixteen *yojana*s.

From the Avīci [hell] down below to the [heaven of the] Paranirmitavaśavartin gods, one calls this the realm of desire. It is thus called because [the beings of this realm] indulge in desire and because their food is in lumps.

The seventeen gods of the realm of form are comprised in the four trances (*dhyāna*). [There are] three gods in the first trance: Brahmakāyika, Brahmapurohita, and Mahābrahma. As for the lifespan of those gods, half a *kalpa* for the Brahmakāyikas, one *kalpa* for the Brahmapurohitas, and one and a half *kalpa*s for the

Mahābrahmas. The bodies of those gods measure half a *yojana,* one *yojana,* and one and a half *yojana*s respectively.

[There are] three gods in the second trance: Parittābha, Apramāṇābha, and Ābhāsvara. As for the lifespan of those gods, two *kalpa*s for the Parittābhas—for the four gods mentioned earlier forty intermediate *kalpa*s are one great *kalpa*, and for the gods who will be mentioned later eighty intermediate *kalpa*s are one great *kalpa*—four *kalpa*s for the Apramāṇābhas, and eight *kalpa*s for the Ābhāsvaras. The bodies of those gods measure two *yojana*s for the Parittābhas, four *yojana*s for the Apramāṇābhas, and eight *yojana*s for the Ābhāsvaras.

[There are] three gods in the third trance: Parittaśubha, Apramāṇaśubha, and Śubhakṛtsna. As for the lifespan of these gods, sixteen *kalpa*s for the Parittaśubhas, thirty-two *kalpa*s for the Apramāṇaśubhas, and sixty-four *kalpa*s for the Śubhakṛtsnas. The bodies of those gods measure sixteen *yojana*s for the Parittaśubhas, thirty-two *yojana*s for the Apramāṇaśubhas, and sixty-four *yojana*s for the Śubhakṛtsnas.

[There are] eight gods in the fourth trance: Anabhraka, Puṇyaprasava, and Bṛhatphala—these three are dwellings for the common; Avṛha, Atapa, Sudṛśa, Sudarśana, and Akaniṣṭha—these five are dwellings for the noble, called the five pure abodes. As for the lifespan of these gods, it is one hundred and twenty-five *kalpa*s for the Anabhrakas, two hundred and fifty *kalpa*s for the Puṇyaprasavas, five hundred *kalpa*s for the Bṛhatphalas, one thousand *kalpa*s for the Avṛhas, two thousand *kalpa*s for the Atapas, four thousand *kalpa*s for the Sudṛśas, eight thousand *kalpa*s for the Sudarśanas, and sixteen thousand *kalpa*s for the Akaniṣṭhas. The bodies of these gods measure one hundred and twenty-five *yojana*s for the Anabhrakas, two hundred and fifty *yojana*s for the Puṇyaprasavas, five hundred *yojana*s for the Bṛhatphalas, one thousand *yojana*s for the Avṛhas, two thousand *yojana*s for the Atapas, four thousand *yojana*s for the Sudṛśas, eight thousand *yojana*s for the Sudarśanas and sixteen thousand *yojana*s for the Akaniṣṭhas.

From Brahmakāyika to Akaniṣṭha, this is all said to be of the
230c realm of form, because [the beings of this realm] are free from desire but not free from matter. So they are said to be of the realm of form.

The four gods of the realm of non-form do not have corporeal form, nor do they have an abode. Because of meditative attainment one distinguishes four: Ākāśānantyāyatana ("Sphere of Unlimited Space"), Vijñānānantyāyatana ("Sphere of Unlimited Consciousness"), Ākiṃcanyāyatana ("Sphere of Nothingness"), and Naivasaṃjñānāsaṃjñāyatana ("Sphere of Neither Identification nor Nonidentification"). As for the lifespan of these gods, twenty thousand great *kalpa*s is the lifespan of Ākāśānantyāyatana, forty thousand great *kalpa*s for Vijñānānantyāyatana, sixty thousand great *kalpa*s for Ākiṃcanyāyatana, and eighty thousand great *kalpa*s for Naivasaṃjñānāsaṃjñāyatana. Those four spheres are said to be the realm of non-form. They are not without certain matter but they are without any coarse matter. So they have no name-and-form (*nāmarūpa*). For the duration of their lifetime one uses the periods year and *kalpa*.

What about their duration? The shortest duration is called *kṣaṇa* (instant). One hundred and twenty *kṣaṇa*s are one *tatkṣaṇa* (second). Sixty *tatkṣaṇa*s are one *lava* (minute). Thirty *lava*s are one *muhūrta*—this is called "a while"; thirty *muhūrta*s are one night-and-day. Thirty night-and-days are one month. Twelve months are one year.[22] There are six kinds of *kalpa*s: 1) an intermediate *kalpa* (*antarakalpa*), which may also be called a separate *kalpa*, 2) an origination *kalpa* (*vivartakalpa*), 3) a continuance *kalpa* (*sthitikalpa*), 4) a destruction *kalpa* (*saṃvartakalpa*), 5) an empty *kalpa* (*śūnyakalpa*), and 6) a great *kalpa* (*mahākalpa*).

First, an intermediate *kalpa*: when the [lifespan of] people in Jambu[dvīpa] gradually decreases in time from immeasurable years to eighty thousand years, this comprises an origination *kalpa*. When [their lifespan] decreases from eighty thousand years to ten years, it is called the initial intermediate *kalpa*. When it increases again to eighty thousand years and decreases to ten years, it is one "round." When such [rounds of] decrease and increase happen eighteen times, they are eighteen intermediate *kalpa*s. But when it reaches for the last time from ten years to eighty thousand years, it is the final end of the intermediate *kalpa*s. The beginning, the end, and the eighteen rounds in between are twenty intermediate *kalpa*s.

Second, an origination *kalpa:* starting from the circle of wind till a sentient being is reborn in the Avīci hell. The inanimate world is completed in an intermediate *kalpa*, as explained earlier. As for the animate world, after the destruction by fire of this trichiliocosm, it originates [again].

When the life of a celestial being from the Ābhāsvara gods had ended, he was reborn in the place of Mahābrahma. All alone and weary, he cried out, "Why couldn't someone with the same fate be reborn in this world?" Such were his thoughts. Although it was not through the power of his thinking, people's lives from the Ābhāsvara heaven ended and they were immediately reborn in that place. The one who was first reborn made this consideration in his mind: "They are reborn because of my longing." And so all in the world call their ancestor Mahābrahma. Then they were successively reborn among the Brahmapurohitas, the Brahmakāyikas, the Paranirmitavaśavartins, and so forth until the Four [Great Heavenly] Kings. They were successively reborn in the continent Kuru to the north, the continent Godānīya to the west, the continent Videha to the east, and the continent Jambu[dvīpa] to the south.

The people of the continent Jambu[dvīpa] then lived for innumerable years. They lived on bliss and were complete with form and mind. Their bodies were luminous and they could freely ascend into the sky. Just like the gods of the realm of form, such was their kind. Earth-essence was gradually produced. Its taste was sweet and its color white, just like honey. Its aroma was fragrant. Then
there was a person who was by nature addicted to its flavor. When 231a
he smelled its fragrance, desire arose. He tried it and ate it, and he also informed others, who subsequently imitated him and took the food. Because they had eaten the food [that was] in lumps, the

luminosity of their bodies disappeared. Through the influence of the actions of the crowd the sun and moon came out, shining in the four [great] continents. Then, when the earth-essence had vanished, there further appeared earth-cakes. Their taste was sweet and their color red, like honey. The [people] were striving to eat [this food]. When the earth-cakes had disappeared too, there then appeared wild creepers. Because they were striving to eat [this food], the wild creepers disappeared too. There appeared natural wild rice for which they had not ploughed or sown. The people all took this food, but because this food was coarse the impurities left over were all secreted through the organs. They all ate from time to time then, choosing the fragrant rice to eat. Later, there were people who were lazy by nature. They constantly took the fragrant rice and hoarded it as their food. The others also imitated this and the fragrant wild rice disappeared. So they all divided the fields, taking precautions not to use up [the food] in the future. They were parsimonious and protective of their own fields [while being] fond and covetous of others' fields. So they started fighting.

Then they all agreed on a virtuous one and appointed him as lord of the fields. Because he was approved by all, he was called King Mahāsaṃmata ("Approved by All"). The king had many sons, who successively succeeded to the throne. The eldest was called Roca. His son was Emperor Kalyāṇa. His son was Varakalyāṇa. His son was Upoṣadha. These are namely the five kings of the origination *kalpa*.

The son of King Upoṣadha was called Mūrdhāta. His son was Emperor Cāru. His son was Upacāru. His son was Cārumat, whose son was Cārumanta. These are namely the five universal monarchs.

The son of King Cārumanta was called Emperor Muci. His son was Mucilinda. His son was Śakuni. His son was Kuśi. His son was Sudarśana. His son was Mahāsudarśana. His son was Vāmaka. His son was Suvarṇa. His son was Bhavya. His son was Bhṛgu. His son was Meru. His son was Nyaṅku. His son was Praṇāda. His son was Mahāpraṇāda. His son was Śaṅkara. His son was Diśaṃpati. His son was Sureṇu. His son was Bharata. His son was Mahādeva.

The lineage of this king had five thousand inheritors. The last son of these had seven thousand inheritors, called Aśmaka kings. The last son had eight thousand inheritors, called Kaurava kings. The last son of these was called King Kapāla. There were nine thousand kings [after him], and the last son was called Geya. There were ten thousand kings [after him] and the last son was Tāmralipta. The last son of fifteen thousand was called Gautama.

Here then was the posterity of Ikṣvāku. That son was the inheritor, and the lineage of King Ikṣvāku numbered one thousand and one hundred. The last son of these, a king in the lineage of Ikṣvāku, was called Virūḍhaka (an Aikṣvāka king). The king had four sons. The first was called Ulkāmukha. The second was called Karakarṇaka. The third was called Hastiniyaṃsa, and the fourth was called Nūpura. They are called the Śākyas.

Nūpura had a son called Nūpurapada. His son was Vasiṣṭha. 231b
His son was Goṣṭha. His son was King Siṃhahanu, who had four sons. One was called Śuddhodana. The second was called Śuklodana. The third was called Droṇodana, and the fourth was called Amṛtodana. The son of King Śuddhodana was the Bhagavat. The second one was called Nanda.

King Śuklodana had two sons. One was called Tiṣyadatta and the other was called Nandika. King Droṇodana had two sons. One was called Aniruddha and the other was called Bhadrika. King Amṛtodana had two sons. One was called Ānanda, and the other was called Devadatta. The son of the Bhagavat was called Rāhula. The Śākya lineage ends here, but kings of other families relied on the doctrine and promoted the teaching.

Two hundred years after the *parinirvāṇa* of the Tathāgata there was a king in the country of Central India, called Aśoka. He was a Dharma King in Jambudvīpa, ruling over its greater part. He was the patron at the time of the middle (second) [Buddhist] council, and he promoted the Buddha's teaching. Three hundred years later, in the northwest of Jambudvīpa, there was a king called Kaniṣka. He was the patron at the time of the third [Buddhist] council and he widely promoted the Buddha's teaching. All the

Dharma Kings of the land of Brahmanical India, the land of Kaśmīra, the land of Khotan, Kučā (pronounced *qiuci*), the land of Nepal, the land of China, the land of Dali,[23] the land of Xixia,[24] and so on, each promoted the Buddha's doctrine in their land.

More than a thousand years after the Tathāgata's *parinirvāṇa,* in the land of Tibet there first was a king called gÑa'-khri btsan-po. After twenty-six generations there was a king called lHa-tho-tho-ri sñan-btsan. At that time the Buddha's teaching first arrived. Five generations later there was a king called Sroṅ-btsan sgam-po.[25] A *paṇḍita* called Ānanda and a translator called Thon-mi Saṃbhoṭa translated the teaching then. He constructed pure abodes in places such as Lhasa, and spread the teaching. Five generations later there was a king called Khri-sroṅ lde-btsan.[26] This king invited the great teacher Śāntarakṣita, the superior master Padmasaṃbhava, the *paṇḍita* Kamalaśīla, and a multitude of *siddha*s. They translated the teaching together with the seven men Vairocanarakṣita, Nāgendrarakṣita, and so on. Other *paṇḍita*s extensively translated the teaching together with the translators (*lotsāva*s), and the three kinds of restraint[27] spread in the land.

Three generations later there was a king called Khri Ral-pa-can. This king's realm was wide. Then there were the *paṇḍita*s Jinamitra and Śīlendrabodhi, and others. Together with Mañjuśrīvarman, Nāgadhvaja from Cog-ro, and so on, they revised the earlier translations and translated what was not yet translated, spreading the teaching far and wide. The lineage of Tibetan kings still exists now. The *paṇḍita*s, translators and chief translators, and the multitude of virtuous friends are quite numerous. That is why the teaching flourishes.

In the land of Northern Mongolia, as the fruition of his pre-
231c vious merits had ripened, a king called Čingis was born. At first Čingis began from the neighboring regions and ruled over many countries of different languages, just as an iron-wheel king. His son was called Ögödäi,[28] who then was named Qaγan. He succeeded him to the imperial throne. His realm became more extensive than

before. He had a son called Güyük, who succeeded him to the imperial throne.

Emperor Čiṅggis's younger son was called Tolui. Tolui's eldest son was called Möngkä, who also succeeded to the royal throne. The king's younger brother was called Qubilai.[29] He succeeded to the imperial throne, subdued various territories, and his realm was very wide. He took refuge in the Buddha's teaching, and converted his people, relying on the doctrine. The Buddha's teaching became twice as great as before and its light was plentiful.

The emperor had three sons. His eldest son was Jiṅ-gim,[30] as wealthy as heaven and adorned with the precious Dharma. His second son was Maṅgala, and his third son was Nomogan. Each had his own virtues, and the same applies to their posterity. Thus it was, beginning from the royal lineage of the Śākyas up to the present royal lineage.

End of the Treatise on the Elucidation of the Knowable, *Fascicle One*

Fascicle Two

The first king and ancestor was King Saṃmata. At that time the fields were divided and [beings] started appropriating each other's property. For the first time they committed theft. When interrogated by the king, they said that they had never stolen, and for the first time they lied. When they were put to death by the king's law, there was killing. Unwholesome factors came into existence.

The beings then performed unwholesome factors, and after their lives had ended they were reborn as animals. They were subsequently reborn as hungry ghosts and were eventually reborn in hell. As soon as one being was reborn in the Avīci hell, then the origination *kalpa* ended.

And so the beings committed many unwholesome acts. Their lifespan gradually decreased and their pleasures dwindled. The lifetime of someone in Jambudvīpa was eighty thousand years, and when a being was reborn in the Avīci hell, he too lived for the same period. So the origination of the animate world takes nineteen intermediate *kalpa*s. The origination of the inanimate world takes one intermediate *kalpa*. And so the origination *kalpa* takes twenty intermediate *kalpa*s.

When people in Jambudvīpa lived eighty thousand years, the continuance *kalpa* began. The continuance *kalpa* also lasts twenty intermediate *kalpa*s. When [the lifespan of beings decreases to] ten years the calamity of weapons begins, [lasting] only seven nights and days. The calamity of sickness begins [and lasts] for seven months and seven days. The calamity of famine begins [and lasts] for seven years, seven months, and seven days. Most [beings]
had died, but when the remaining ones catch sight of one another, 232a
they raise thoughts of longing. They are fond of each other and stay away from killing. As they eventually produce what is wholesome, the length of their lifespan and their pleasures again increase to fully eighty thousand years. When they increase, the universal

monarchs appear, converting the people, relying on the doctrine. When they decrease, the Bhagavat appears and saves the beings. During both [periods of] increase and decrease Solitary Buddhas (*pratyekabuddhas*) appear in the world. They form a field of merit for sentient beings.

The continuance *kalpa* also lasts twenty intermediate *kalpas*. As soon as the destruction *kalpa* begins, the animate world is destroyed. No sentient being is reborn in the Avīci hell. When the actions of a previous life have ended, they are reborn in another destination. Those for whom they have not ended yet are reborn in a higher hell, or they are reborn in hells in other worlds. When the Avīci hell is empty, in the same way the higher hells gradually become empty. When they are reborn in the destination of the hungry ghosts, in the same way the destinations of a hungry ghost or an animal become empty. Those in the human destination, except the people of Kuru, and also the desiring gods follow their Dharma-nature, without any teacher. When they have obtained the first trance (*dhyāna*), they are reborn among the gods of the first trance. When the people of Kuru to the north are reborn among the gods of the realm of desire and have obtained the first trance, they are reborn among the gods of the first trance. Without any teacher and following their Dharma-nature, they, having obtained the second trance, are reborn among the gods of the second trance. When [everything] from the Avīci hell to the Brahma world becomes empty, it goes on in this way for nineteen intermediate *kalpas* too.

After that seven suns arise in the four [great] continents. The first [appears] where no rain falls. All medicinal herbs and orchards wither away. When the second sun appears, ditches and ponds dry up. When the third sun appears, the Ganges River [and other rivers] all dry up. When the fourth sun appears, Lake Anavatapta goes dry. When the fifth sun appears, the water of the ocean sinks to knee-high. When the sixth sun appears, the great ocean goes dry too. When the seventh sun appears, the inanimate world is stirred up by a heap of fire. [Everything] from the Avīci hell straight up to the Brahma world is destroyed by fire. [This] lasts one intermediate *kalpa*.

The destruction *kalpa* altogether lasts twenty intermediate *kalpa*s. The same applies to an empty *kalpa*. In this way, [the *kalpa*s of] origination, continuance, destruction, and emptiness last eighty *kalpa*s. These eighty altogether are called one great *kalpa*. This is the length of the lifespan of the Brahmakāyikas and so on.

The destruction of the inanimate world is threefold: by fire, water, and wind. The destruction is as explained earlier. After seven such times, the world originates again. It is then destroyed by water, up to the second trance (*dhyāna*) heaven. In the Ābhāsvara heaven big clouds appear. They bring torrential rains and the inanimate world completely dissolves, just as when water melts salt. That water naturally dries up, and after one water calamity again occur seven fire calamities. After seven fire calamities there again comes one water [calamity]. And so, when the water calamities fully reach seven times, there further are seven fire calamities, after which the world originates.

It is destroyed by a wind calamity, up to the third trance (*dhyāna*) heaven. When the force of the wind blows away Mount Meru, how much more will it do so to the other [mountains]! Although the fourth trance heaven is free from any outside calamity, those sentient beings are born together with a [heavenly] palace, and when their life ends the palace disappears. Thus the animate and the inanimate worlds, as well as origination, destruction, and so on, are all explained.

Dependent Origination

Next, the law of dependent origination (*pratītyasamutpāda*) in a 232b
series of causes and their fruitions. Because causes and conditions arise in mutual dependence, one uses the term dependent origination. Dependent origination is twofold: external dependent origination and internal dependent origination. External dependent

origination is the way of the completion of the world, just like seeds bringing forth sprouts, as explained before. [As for] internal dependent origination, if there is ignorance, there are formations and so on. This is called progressive (*anuloma*) dependent origination. If ignorance is extinguished, formations and so on are [also] extinguished. This is called retrogressive (*pratiloma*) dependent origination.

Progressive dependent origination is sevenfold. In succession, [the seven types are:] 1) situational (*āvasthika*), 2) continuing (*prākarṣika*), 3) serial (*sāṃbandhika*), 4) instantaneous (*kṣaṇika*), 5) consisting of the three periods of time (*trayo'ntika*), 6) consisting of two sets of cause and result (*ubhayato hetuphala*), and 7) consisting of three defilements (*saṃkleśasaṃgraha*).

[First,] situational [progressive dependent origination] is the situational five aggregates (*skandha*s) that share in the defilements [committed] in previous births. They are [collectively] called ignorance (*avidyā*). As ignorance is preponderant, they are so called. All the following take their name from a preponderance. The factors—formations and so on—all have the five aggregates. Formations (*saṃskāra*) are the situational five aggregates of the wholesome and unwholesome actions committed in previous worlds. Consciousness (*vijñāna*) is the situational five aggregates at one moment, exactly when they make a connection with life in the mother's womb. Name-and-form (*nāmarūpa*) are the situational five aggregates after the consciousness that makes a connection with life and before the six [sense] bases arise. Name: the four aggregates—feeling, identification, formation, and consciousness—are called name. Form: the situation when dwelling in the womb. The five: *kalala* ("combination" or "condensation"), *arbuda* ("a swelling"), *peśī* ("a lump of flesh"), *ghana* ("solid"), and *praśākhā* (the body, limbs, and muscles are produced) are [collectively] called form. The six [sense] bases (*ṣaḍāyatana*): the situational five aggregates, when the eyes and so on are produced while yet in the mother's womb, to the extent that the three (sense faculty, sense object, and sense conciousness) are combined, although one does not completely distinguish the objects yet. Contact (*sparśa*): the situational five aggregates when the three—[sense] faculty, [sense] object, and [sense] consciousness—are combined, although one cannot yet completely distinguish the cause of suffering (*duḥkha*) and happiness. Feeling (*vedanā*): the situational five aggregates when understanding the three feelings and the different characteristics of their causes, although as an infant one cannot be lascivious yet. Craving (*tṛṣṇā*): the situational five aggregates when one can complete lascivious desire in the prime of life, although one does not pursue it extensively. Grasping (*upādāna*): the situational five aggregates when searching everywhere in order to obtain all sorts of splendid property. Existence (*bhava*): the situational five aggregates when, because of one's search, one accumulates actions that implicate a future fruition. Birth (*jāti*): the situational five aggregates when through the power of these actions one has lost one's life here and is connected only with a future existence. Old age and death (*jarāmaraṇa*): the situational five aggregates from name-and-form to feeling [leading to] a future birth.

The Sarvāstivādins say that situational [progressive] dependent origination is the same as the continuing and the serial [kinds of progressive dependent origination]. The Sautrāntika school does not have a theory of situational [progressive dependent origination].[31]

As for continuing [progressive dependent origination], ignorance is the opposite of knowledge. It is a mental factor, the cause of the bringing about of formations. Formation is the action that has been brought about—good, bad, or neutral actions. Consciousness: induced by actions, consciousness is produced. Name-and-form is the five aggregates in the womb. The six [sense] bases: the faculties of the eye, and so on are produced. Contact is when the combination of the three—[sense] faculty, [sense] object, and 232c
[sense] consciousness—is distinguished. It is a mental factor. Feeling is the suffering, happiness, or equanimity caused thereby.

Craving is attachment to the object of happiness. Grasping is seeking after that object. Existence is brought about thereby, and one performs actions [that bring about] a future birth. Birth is connected with life through the series of actions. Old age and death lead to rebirth in another life, and at the end one will die again.

The same applies to serial [progressive dependent origination].

Instantaneous [progressive dependent origination]: in one instant dependent origination with its twelve links of existence is completed. When someone kills out of covetousness, the delusion is called ignorance. The interruption of life is formation. The distinction of the objects is called consciousness. As the five aggregates are equally present, one uses the general term name-and-form. The faculties that reside in name-and-form are called the six [sense] bases. When the three—[sense] faculty, [sense] object, and [sense] consciousness—are combined there is contact. Because of contact [there is feeling]. The covetousness is craving. The ties associated with it are called grasping. The two actions, corporeal and verbal, that arise are called existence. The accumulation of such factors is called birth. Maturation is called old age, and extinction is called death.

[Progressive dependent origination] consisting of the three periods: ignorance and formation are comprised in the past and they are called causal links. The five links, consciousness and so on, are comprised in the present and they are called resultant links. The three, craving, grasping, and existence, are comprised in the present and they are called causal links for the future. Birth and old age and death are comprised in the future and they are called resultant links. Past—two links; present—eight links; future—two links. So, twelve links.

[Progressive dependent origination] consisting of two sets of cause and result: these are double, anterior and posterior. Anterior: ignorance is a defilement, and formation is an action. These two are causal links. The five links, consciousness and so on, brought about thereby are resultant links. [They are] one set of cause and result. The two links, craving and grasping in the present, are defilements and existence is an action. The three are causes for the future. The future birth and old age and death, brought about thereby, are resultant links. [They are] one set of cause and result. And so the twelve links of existence consist of two sets of cause and result.

[Progressive dependent origination] consisting of three defilements: the three—ignorance, craving, and grasping—are defilements. The two—formation and existence—are actions. They are said to be the truth of origination. The seven links—consciousness and so on—are painful. They are said to be the truth of suffering. This is progressive dependent origination.

Retrogressive dependent origination: the extinction of ignorance means the extinction of formation. When ignorance is extinguished one completes the knowledge of selflessness. This is the truth of the path. When ignorance is extinguished, formation, which is the cause of rebirth, is extinguished. As the inducing action is extinguished, the five links—consciousness and so on—are extinguished. Because these are extinguished, that which gives rise to later action, craving, and grasping are extinguished. Because these are extinguished, birth and old age and death are all extinguished too. They are the truth of cessation. We have explained the four truths.[32]

The Five Factors

The animate and the inanimate [worlds], dependent origination, and the four truths are all comprised in the five factors (*dharma*): 1) the factor [of] matter (*rūpa*), 2) the factor [of] awareness (*citta*), 3) the accompanying mental factors (*caitasika*), 4) the dissociated 233a
factors (*viprayukta*), and 5) the unconditioned factors (*asaṃskṛta*).

One: the factor [of] matter is the matter aggregate (*rūpa-skandha*). [It has] eleven factors: five [sense] faculties (*indriya*), five [sense] objects (*viṣaya*), and unmanifest matter (*avijñaptirūpa*). Let us talk about the five [sense] faculties. Particles of the faculty of the eye are like a fragrant coriander flower. They dwell spread out on the pupil of the eye. Particles of the faculty of the ear are like rolled-up birch bark and dwell in the drum of the ear. Particles of the faculty of the nose are like two nails and dwell in the nostrils. Particles of the faculty of the tongue are shaped like a half-moon, spread out on the tongue. Particles of the faculty of the body are like the body's measures too. They are all over the faculty of the body, from head to toe. Because the [sense] faculties consist of [atomic] particles, one cannot take them as objects.

Let us talk about the five [sense] objects [of the factor of matter]. Matter is said to be the object that is taken by the eye. There are two kinds, color and shape. Color is fourfold: bluish green, yellow, red, and white. Shape is sixteenfold: long and short, square and round, high and low, straight and not-straight, shining and shaded, bright and dark, cloudy, smoky, dusty, and foggy. [So matter has] the number twenty. Sound is said to be the object that is taken by the ear. It is twofold: 1) with an organic cause, such as words, and 2) without an organic cause, such as the sound of a drum. Each is twofold, determinate or neutral, making it four. It is further pleasant or unpleasant, the divisions thus adding up to six. Smell is said to be the object that is taken by the nose. It is fourfold: sweet smells and bad smells, and because these are further even or uneven, the divisions make four. Flavor is the object that is said to be taken by the tongue. It is sixfold: sweet, sour, bitter, pungent, salty, or bland. The tangible is the object that is said to be taken by the body. The causal tangibles are the four great elements, and the resultant tangibles are smooth and rough, heavy and light, cold and hot, and hunger and thirst.

Talking about unmanifest matter, it namely consists of restraint, non-restraint, and matter that is neither of the two. This is the matter aggregate.

The second factor is awareness. It is sixfold: eye-consciousness, ear-consciousness, nose-consciousness, tongue-consciousness, body-consciousness, and mind-consciousness. These six are the consciousness aggregate (*vijñānaskandha*).

The third factor is the accompanying mental factors. They number forty-six. First are the generally permeating factors (*mahābhūmika*), of which there are ten. 1) Feeling (*vedanā*) is experiencing. 2) Identification (*saṃjñā*) lets an awareness grasp its object. 3) Volition (*cetanā*) makes awareness move. 4) Attention (*manaskāra*) lets awareness follow its object. 5) Resolve (*adhimukti*) makes awareness certain of its object. This mainly means that one lets one's awareness be free from weakness regarding the object it follows. 6) Interest (*chanda*) is application. 7) Contact (*sparśa*) is a combination while scrutinizing the object. 8) Wisdom (*prajñā*) is analyzing. 9) Mindfulness (*smṛti*) makes awareness clearly recollect and not forget its object. 10) Concentration (*samādhi*) makes awareness focus on one object. Such ten are universal with every awareness. They are called the generally permeating factors.

Second, the good generally permeating factors (*kuśalamahābhūmika*) [also] number ten. 1) Faith (*śraddhā*) makes awareness pure regarding its object. 2) Heedfulness (*apramāda*) is the constant practice of good qualities and the preservation of one's mind. 3) Tranquility (*praśrabdhi*) is the patient acceptance of awareness. 4) Equanimity (*upekṣā*) makes awareness even. 5) Shame (*hrī*) is staying respectful toward all qualities and the virtuous. 6) Modesty (*apatrāpya*) is fear of sinful views. 7) Absence of greed (*alobha*) is having no attachment to what is impure. 8) Absence of hatred 233b
(*adveṣa*) is having no happiness in causing damage to any living being. 9) Nonviolence (*avihiṃsā*) is feeling pity for living beings, so that they are not harmed. 10) Energy (*vīrya*) makes awareness brave concerning what is good. Such ten are universal with every good awareness. They are called the good generally permeating factors.[33]

Third, the defiled generally permeating factors (*kleśamahābhūmika*) are sixfold. 1) Delusion (*moha*) is foolishness, namely ignorance, absence of knowledge, and absence of clarity. 2) Heedlessness (*pramāda*) is carelessness, not developing any good qualities. 3) Sloth (*kausīdya*) is laziness, the lack of mental courage.

4) Absence of faith (*āśraddhya*) is mental impurity. 5) Lethargy (*styāna*) is the absence of patient acceptance in a corporeal or mental series. It means obscurity and heaviness. 5) Excitability (*auddhatya*) is the restlessness of awareness. The above six are universal with defiled awareness. They are called the defiled generally permeating factors.[34]

Fourth, the bad generally permeating factors (*akuśalamahābhūmika*) are twofold. 1) Shamelessness (*āhrīkya*) makes awareness disrespectful toward any qualities and the virtuous. 2) Disregard (*anapatrāpya*)—one is not fearful of anything sinful. These two are universal with every bad awareness. They are called the bad generally permeating factors.

Fifth, the factors of limited defiled extent (*parittakleśabhūmika*) are tenfold. 1) Anger (*krodha*) causes exasperation. 2) Vengefulness (*upanāha*) is constantly pondering over one's object of anger, unremittingly contracting hatred. 3) Craftiness (*śāṭhya*) is deviousness. 4) Deceit (*māyā*) is to fool others. 5) Envy (*īrṣyā*) is when one cannot stand another's virtue. 6) Spite (*pradāśa*) is when one tightly clings to any evil, and therefore does not accept any fitting reproval. 7) Hypocrisy (*mrakṣa*) is hiding one's [own] evil. 8) Selfishness (*mātsarya*) makes one parsimonious regarding one's lawful possessions. 9) Arrogance (*mada*) is attachment to one's own beauty and strength, to one's family, and so on, so that one is overbearing. 10) Violence (*vihiṃsā*) is bringing pressure to bear on others. These ten can only be abandoned through spiritual practice. They are universal in the stage of mental consciousness, and they are called factors of limited defiled extent.

Sixth, the indeterminate factors (*aniyata*) are eightfold. 1) Initial thought (*vitarka*) is characterized by a coarse mental process regarding an object. 2) Sustained thought (*vicāra*) is characterized by a subtle mental process regarding an object. 3) Regret (*kaukṛtya*) means that one regrets an evil action that has been committed. 4) Sleepiness (*middha*) is the inability to control one's corporeal and mental series, so that one's awareness is drowsy. 5) Repugnance (*pratigha*) makes one's awareness enjoy harming living beings.

6) Attachment (*rāga*) is thirsting after the impure. 7) Pride (*māna*) makes one haughty. 8) Perplexity (*vicikitsā*) makes one uncertain. Because these eight kinds are indeterminate in any of the aforementioned stages, they are called indeterminate.

The *Abhidharmasamuccaya* (*Treatise on the Compendium of Scholastics*) and the *Pañcaskandhaka* (*Treatise on the Five Aggregates*) explain eleven good [factors]: [add] inner realization of the four truths, called absence of delusion. As for defiled attention and resolve, holding impurity as purity among secondary defilements, one uses the term wrong attention and wrong resolve among the fundamental defilements. That which is part of defiled wisdom, holding perverted views and conjecturing about any truth, is called incorrect comprehension. Among the secondary defilements, that which is part of defiled mindfulness, being unable to clearly remember any object, is called forgetfulness. That which is part of defiled concentration, letting awareness about any object stray, is called distraction. The *Abhidharmakośa* (*Treatise on the* 233c
Storehouse of Scholastics) does not have such a theory.

The above are the mental factors. Except for the two, feeling and identification, they are all comprised in the formation aggregate. This ends [the discussion] of the [forty-six] mental factors.

There are fourteen kinds of dissociated formations (*viprayukta-saṃskāra*). In a [mental] series of sentient beings the possession of something else, associated with restraint, is called acquisition (*prāpti*). The possession of something else, not associated with that restraint, is called nonacquisition (*aprāpti*). When the species of sentient beings act in the same way, it is called the likeness of beings (*sattvasabhāgatā*). If one is born in the heaven of the sentient beings who do not have conceptual identification, there is a factor that can make awareness and its concomitants stop. This substance, which really exists, is called fruition without identification (*āsaṃjñikaphala*).

There further is another factor that can make awareness and its concomitants stop. It is called attainment without identification (*asaṃjñisamāpatti*). Without identification is namely the appellation of the attainment. Or, having attained absence of identification, one uses the term attainment without identification. When identification and feeling in the [mental] series of the noble, as explained below, are extinguished, this really existing substance is called attainment of cessation (*nirodhasamāpatti*). As soon as a being is born and while it remains before it dies, one uses the term faculty life (*jīvitendriya*). Previously nonexistent but now existing is called birth (*jāti*). What causes a brief stay is called duration (*sthiti*). Change is called old age (*jarā*). Decay is called impermanence (*anityatā*). They are the four characteristic marks of the conditioned (*saṃskṛtalakṣaṇa*).

That which can explain the essence is called the group of words (*nāmakāya*). That which explains the ultimate meaning is called the group of sentences (*padakāya*). The basis of these two is called the group of letters (*vyañjanakāya*). These are the fourteen factors. In this outline of the meaning there further is the disruption of the harmonious sangha, called disharmony. The fruition of the actions one has done matures for oneself, as if one was carrying heavy debts, never unavailing. These things also bind. They are the dissociated formations.

The Sarvāstivādins [say] that the three—matter, awareness, and accompanying factors—are different things. Sautrāntika masters say that those three other factors are falsely said to be different.[35] The forty-six accompanying mental factors, except feeling and identification, and that which is dissociated from [awareness] are called the formation aggregate (*saṃskāraskandha*).[36]

The unconditioned factors [are discussed in Part V, pages 64–5]. Such material factors (*rūpadharma*) may be called the ten elements (*dhātu*), leaving out unmanifest matter. They are ten: eye and so on. The factor [of] awareness has seven elements, the six consciousnesses and the element of the mind faculty. When one explains the bases, those seven factors are comprised by the one base mind (*manas*). The accompanying mental factors, the dissociated factors, the unconditioned factors, and unmanifest matter are all called the element factors. They are also called the base factors.[37]

Such is the explanation of the knowable: the five factors, the five aggregates, the twelve bases, and the eighteen elements.

III. The Factors of the Path

Furthermore, the path. When someone with few desires, who is contented and possesses the nature of a spiritual family,[38] forsakes the miscellaneous objects in body and mind and dwells in lay morality (i.e., an *upāsaka*), he must diligently pursue learning. When he is extensively learned, he should reflect on the meaning of what he has learned. After reflection he must develop himself, that is, he must develop peace and insight. Someone with considerable greed should develop the contemplation of foulness (*aśubhabhāvanā*). Someone with considerable hatred should develop the contemplation of loving-kindness. Someone with considerable delusion should develop the contemplation distinguishing dependent origination. Someone with a considerable ego should develop the contemplation distinguishing the elements (*dhātuvyavasthāna*). Someone with considerable confusion should develop the contemplation counting the breath (*anāpānasmṛti*). After the completion of peace and insight one develops resolve, and so understands in proper order the body, internal and external. This is called the 234a
establishment of mindfulness of the body. One understands in proper order suffering, happiness, and equanimity, which is called the establishment of mindfulness of feeling. One understands in proper order the six consciousnesses and the mental factors, which is called the establishment of mindfulness of awareness. One understands in proper order identification, formation, and the unconditioned, which is called the establishment of mindfulness of the factors. The cultivation of these four factors means accumulation of knowledge.[39] After the path has accumulated this, one develops a path of preparatory application.[40] In the state of heat one abandons the evil already produced, one does not let the unproduced evil be produced, one lets the good already produced increase, and

one lets the unproduced good be produced. Such four factors are called the four right exertions; some texts say right abandonments.

In the state of the summit: the concentration of interest in good factors, the concentration of the effort to rejoice in the good, the concentration of attention to good awareness, and the concentration of investigation into the good. Such are called the four bases of supernatural power.

In the state of patient acceptance: proceeding in worldly perfect enlightenment, the purity is called faith, rejoicing in the cultivation of good factors is called energy, clearly remembering and not forgetting is called mindfulness, special attention to one object is called concentration, and knowing what to take and what to leave is called wisdom. The practice of these five factors produces good factors. Therefore they are called the five faculties. In the state of the highest worldly [factor] one develops the five: faith, energy, mindfulness, concentration, and wisdom. Because they can destroy that which is adverse, they are called the five powers. This is the path of preparatory application.

In the state of the path of vision one perceives the four truths, which is called right view. The motivation for correct words is called right thought. A truthful right explanation is called right speech. Giving up bad actions is called right action. The rejection of a wrong livelihood is called right livelihood. Striving for good factors is called right effort. Clearly remembering and not forgetting is called right mindfulness. Special attention to one object is called right concentration. Such eight factors are called the eight members of the noble path.[41] This is the path of vision.

That which is to be abandoned through the path of vision are the distinct defilements, and also their acquisition and their characteristics.[42] For the truth of suffering in the realm of desire: attachment, repugnance, pride, ignorance, perplexity, belief in a self, extreme view, the view that means attachment to moral precepts and vows, adherence to particular views, and false view. For the two truths, of origination and of cessation, for each one must subtract three views. Seven and seven are fourteen. For those that are abandoned through the truth of the path, subtract the first two views. For the four truths in the realm of desire, this adds up to thirty-two. For the four truths in the realm of form, subtract repugnance for each of them, adding up to twenty-eight. The same applies to the realm of non-form. Thus in the three realms eighty-eight are to be abandoned through the path of vision.

In the state of the spiritual path, clearly remembering good factors is called the member of enlightenment mindfulness. Investigation into what to take and what to leave is called the member of enlightenment wisdom. The search after vigor is called the member of enlightenment energy. The realization of pure joy is called the member of enlightenment joy. Tolerance of body and mind is called the member of enlightenment tranquility. Not being dragged on by worldly factors, being free from attachment and free from impediment, is called the member of enlightenment equanimity. Letting awareness dwell on its object is called the member of enlightenment concentration. The practice of these seven members is called the spiritual path.[43]

That which is to be abandoned through the spiritual path are the innate defilements, their acquisition, and their characteristics. They are neutral, or impure and good. In the realm of desire [there are] four: attachment, repugnance, pride,[44] and ignorance. Each has nine degrees, [making] altogether thirty six. In the first trance (*dhyāna*) in the realm of form, repugnance is left out. The remaining three each are ninefold, making twenty-seven. Thus 234b
the same applies to the second, third, and fourth trances. In the realm of form one has altogether the number one hundred and eight. The same applies to the realm of non-form. Thus, [the defilements] to be abandoned through the spiritual path in the three realms altogether number two hundred and fifty-two.[45]

Then one realizes the ten factors of the adept:[46] right view, right thought, right speech, right action, right livelihood, right effort, right mindfulness, right concentration (i.e., the noble eightfold path), right liberation, and the knowledge of right liberation. This is the path of the adept.

IV. The Factors of Fruition

Furthermore, fruition. As one has generated the awareness [of enlightenment] to deliver oneself from the cycle of existence (samsara) with the thirty-seven factors that are the members of enlightenment,[47] as explained above, one is very swift when possessing keen faculties [and thus] realizes arhatship in three births. In the first birth one develops that which is good, contributing to liberation; [this is] called the path of accumulation. In the second birth one develops that which is good, contributing to intellectual penetration; [this is] called the path of preparatory application.[48] In the third birth one may realize the fourth fruition as a *śramaṇa*. But with dull faculties one will be indolent, as this is not definite.

Concerning the path of the *śramaṇa* (asceticism), one uses the term fruition for the four—progress toward entering the stream, and so on.[49] Progress toward entering the stream happens in the path of preparatory application. That which is comprised by the previous animate and inanimate worlds is all unpleasant by nature. This is the truth of suffering. Furthermore, its cause is actions and defilement. This is the truth of origination. Bringing liberation thereof is the truth of cessation. Furthermore, its cause is the truth of the path. When one's practice is proficient and one gradually realizes the path of vision because of this, one for the first time realizes the truth of suffering,[50] which is fourfold by nature: for change one uses the term impermanent; for the three sufferings[51] one uses the term painful; because that which really exists does not have the same aggregates as a self, one uses the term emptiness; because that which really exists is different from a self, one uses the term selflessness. One intuitively realizes their four knowledges.[52]

Then one realizes the truth of origination, which is fourfold by nature: as one sows causes of suffering, it is a cause; as the cause of suffering is present, it is origination; as a continuation of causes of suffering, it is a source; because it accords with causes of suffering, it is a condition. One intuitively realizes their four knowledges.[53]

Then one realizes the truth of cessation, which is fourfold by nature: because the cause of suffering ceases, it is cessation; because the result of suffering is appeased, it is appeasement; because it surpasses the impure, it is excellent; abandoning the cycle of existence, it means escape. One intuitively realizes their four knowledges.[54]

Then one realizes the truth of the path, which is fourfold by nature: because one proceeds to the meaningful, it is a path; because one is in agreement with the right principles, it is right; because one develops nonconceptual knowledge (*nirvikalpaka jñāna*), it is a mode. One intuitively realizes their three knowledges.[55]

In the [above] fifteen one is said to progress toward the first fruition [of the stream-enterer (*srota-āpanna*)]. As for the sixteenth, because one forever surpasses all existence in this truth of the path, it leads to liberation. One intuitively realizes its one knowledge.[56] With these sixteen one dwells in the first fruition.

Having realized the four truths and their sixteen aspects, one's practice is proficient. When one abandons the first five among the nine degrees of defilement that are to be abandoned through the spiritual path in the realm of desire, one progresses toward once-returning. Abandoning the sixth degree means the fruition of the once-returner (*sakṛdāgāmin*). The once-returner returns to the realm of desire, as he experiences one rebirth. 234c

Because the three remaining degrees may be abandoned in one rebirth in the realm of desire and when, intuitively realizing the aspects, his practice is proficient, one abandons degrees seven and eight, which is called progress toward non-returning. Abandoning the ninth degree is called the fruition of the non-returner (*anāgāmin*). The non-returner has completely abandoned all defilements of the realm of desire. As he will definitely not return to the realm of desire to be reborn and when, intuitively realizing the aspects of the higher realms, his practice is proficient, the nine defilements of each of the four trances (*dhyāna*) and the four immaterial ones are abandoned. The first degree in the first trance is the beginning.

Up to the final abandonment of the eighth degree in the summit of existence,[57] one is called someone who progresses toward arhatship. Having abandoned the ninth degree one uses the term fruition of arhatship. In arhatship one has completely and without any remainder abandoned defilement in the three realms. One is called an arhat.

Scriptural texts[58] say, "The eight [stages]: the stage of bright vision, and so on."[59] The path of accumulation of the disciple is the stage of bright vision. Desire has withered away, and the [sense] faculties and their objects do not meet. The good that is developed is called the stage of bright vision. The stage of the spiritual family is the path of preparatory application. One will not necessarily become a Buddha but one definitely will become one of the spiritual family of the disciples (*śrāvaka*s) or *pratyekabuddha*s. It is called the stage of the spiritual family. The stage of the eighth person means progressing toward the first fruition. Up to the fruition of arhatship one uses the term stage of the eighth person. The stage of vision means one dwells in the first fruition. Because the aspects of the four truths are clearly realized one uses the term stage of vision. The stage of attenuation is the fruition of the once-returner. Because the defilements of the realm of desire have for the most part been abandoned, one uses the term stage of attenuation. The stage of nonattachment is the fruition of the non-returner. Because one is nonattached in the realm of desire, one uses the term stage of nonattachment. The skilled stage is arhatship. When suffering is known and its origination is abandoned, when cessation is realized and the path is practiced, one uses the term skilled stage. The stages of the disciples (*śrāvaka*s) are [that of] the once-returner,[60] the non-returner, and the arhat. These three are called stages of the disciple.

The stage of the *pratyekabuddha:* with the aforementioned thirty-seven factors that are the members of enlightenment,[61] one wishes to realize *bodhi* (enlightenment) all by oneself. Thus one generates the awareness [of enlightenment] and practices [the thirty-seven factors of enlightenment] for a hundred great *kalpa*s.

With one's last body one is reborn in a world without a Buddha. Not making use of the teaching of a master, one completes the realization of solitary enlightenment (i.e., *pratyekabuddha*). This is twofold: [like a] unicorn, and living with a group. One who is like a unicorn lives all alone, possessing noble virtuous behavior. The [second] kind who lives with a group stays with a group of people.

The final perfect Buddha: in order to become Buddha with the aforementioned thirty-seven factors that are the members of enlightenment for the sake of all sentient beings, he has produced great compassion and the excellent awareness of *bodhi* (*bodhicitta*). He has served the Buddhas, so that they may all rejoice. For the sake of others he has practiced the practice of the six perfections (*pāramitās*)[62] during three incalculable *kalpas*, finally becoming a Buddha.

Śākyamuni, the Tathāgata, once was a potter named Mahāprabha. In the place of Mahāśākya Tathāgata he for the first time generated the awareness [of enlightenment]. During the first incalculable *kalpa* he served seventy-five thousand Buddhas. The last Buddha was called Ratnaśikhin. During the second incalculable 235a
kalpa he served seventy-six thousand Buddhas. The last Buddha was called Dīpaṃkara. During the third incalculable *kalpa* he served seventy-seven thousand Buddhas. The last Buddha was called Vipaśyin.

The six perfections: because of his great compassion for all living beings he kindly gave all his belongings away. When he was Crown Prince Viśvāṃtara he utterly completed the *pāramitā* of giving (*dāna*). When he was not yet without attachment his limbs were cut off, but he did not feel the least anger. When he was the seer Kṣāntivādin, his practice of the two [*pāramitās* of] patience (*kṣānti*) and [of] morality (*śīla*) was utterly perfect. When he was the son of a *brāhmaṇa* he saw the Buddha Tiṣya dwelling in the concentration of the element fire and he circumambulated for seven nights and days, forgetting to put down one foot. While he was making his rounds, [Tiṣya] said, "Neither in the heavens nor on earth, neither in these realms nor in the abode of Vaiśravaṇa, nor in any place of the gods, going to their palaces, nor in any of the ten directions is there such a man, a bull king, a great *śramaṇa*. Searching the land and the forests in the mountains, nowhere is your equal."

Being praised in this way, he crossed nine *kalpa*s and his *pāramitā* of energy (*vīrya*) was utterly completed. When he was dwelling on his adamantine seat in the place of perfection, at dusk he subdued Māra's crowd, and at dawn he entered the diamond-like concentration. His practice of the two, concentration (*samādhi*) and wisdom (*prajñā*), was utterly completed. Thus he sat on the adamantine seat. Before he subdued Māra he had developed enough merit and knowledge during three incalculable *kalpa*s. He had served the Buddhas and, although he had completed the six perfections, he was an ordinary person (*pṛthagjana*). Sitting on his adamantine seat he realized the paths of vision and of spiritual development, realizing perfect enlightenment. In the vehicle of the disciples[63] at the time of causality they do not assert an understanding of the factors as egoless and void, compassion, the practice of giving as tripartite,[64] emptiness, or the aspects of the ten stages.[65] At the time of fruition they do not assert the enjoyment body (*saṃbhogakāya*), nor the four wisdoms.[66]

The factor of perfect enlightenment is comprised by six—the body, knowledge, abandonment, benefiting others, great compassion, and the possession of qualities. There are two bodies, the material body (*rūpakāya*), and the Dharma body (*dharmakāya*). The material body is the natural body, which has the thirty-two primary and the eighty secondary marks. In order to save the *gandharva*s or Pilindavatsa, he appeared as a *gandharva* king or as a noble universal monarch. This is the transformation body. But the size of the natural bodies of the Buddhas, their age and fields, and their faculties were different in various kinds of ways. The Dharma body has the ten factors of the adept.[67] It is the same for all the Buddhas.

There are two knowledges, full knowledge (*parijñāna*) and right knowledge (*saṃprajāna*). Full knowledge is namely awareness of the aggregates, the elements, the bases, and the nature of cause and result. That is why it is called full knowledge. Right knowledge is namely awareness of the factors of impermanence and so on in the four truths. That is why it is called right knowledge.

There are two abandonments, abandonment of the obstruction of defilements, and abandonment of the obstruction of the knowable. Abandonment of the obstruction of defilements namely reme- 235b
dies the fundamental defilements of attachment and so on, and also the secondary defilements,[68] so that they are abandoned. Abandonment of the obstruction of the knowable namely remedies the obstructions—the object, the right time, and the factor of ignorance of something specific—so that they are abandoned. Benefiting others is twofold: establishing liberation for all sentient beings, rejecting that which is offensive so that they may dwell in the path; and establishing a good destination for all sentient beings, rejecting evil so that they may dwell in what is good. Great compassion and the qualities will presently be explained.

The noble ones have said that there are eleven kinds of qualities: 1) dispassion (*araṇa*), 2) knowledge resulting from resolve (*praṇidhijñāna*), 3) the four discriminations (*pratisaṃvid*), 4) the six higher faculties (*abhijñā*), 5) the four trances (*dhyāna*), 6) the four immaterial ones (*ārūpya*), 7) the four immeasurables (*apramāṇa*), 8) the eight liberations (*vimokṣa*), 9) the ten all-bases (*kṛtsnāyatana*), 10) the eight spheres of mastery (*abhibhāyatana*), and 11) the three concentrations (*samādhi*s).

Dispassion: on the basis of awareness in the fourth trance one wishes that no being would take their own person as an object and bring forth any defilement. Because his reflection is concentrated one uses the term dispassion.

Knowledge resulting from resolve: on the basis of awareness in the fourth trance one's resolve is considered to be first. It leads to the rise of such knowledge. Because one gains knowledge according to one's resolve, one uses the term knowledge resulting from resolve.

The four discriminations: 1) discrimination of factors, because one knows the names of the factors; 2) discrimination of the meaning, because one exactly knows the meaning; 3) discrimination of language, because one exactly knows the words; and 4) discrimination of perspicuity, because one exactly knows the right principles. They are called the four discriminations.

The six higher faculties: 1) knowledge of the base of supernatural power, because one may roam unhindered through precipices; 2) knowledge of the divine ear, because one knows all different sounds, whether near or far; 3) knowledge of the divine eye, because, as one sees fit one can take in what has been screened off—the forms in all directions, very small or far away; 4) knowledge of the mental make-up of others, because one knows whether or not the awarenesses of others have desire; 5) knowledge of previous existences, because one knows the things in the former lives of oneself and others; and 6) knowledge of the destruction of impurities, because one knows all paths, mundane or supramundane. The first five [of the above six] are impure, based on the fourth trance. The sixth is pure, because it is based on the ninth [stage].[69]

The four trances (*dhyāna*): in the first trance one has five members: 1) initial thought, 2) sustained thought, 3) joy, 4) happiness, and 5) undivided attention. In the second trance one has four members: 1) inner serenity, 2) joy, 3) happiness, and 4) undivided attention. In the third trance one has five members: 1) equanimity, 2) right mindfulness, 3) tranquility, 4) the experience of happiness, and 5) undivided attention. In the fourth trance one has four members: 1) pure equanimity, 2) pure mindfulness, 3) the experience of neither suffering nor happiness, and 4) undivided attention.

235c The four immaterial ones: because when developing application one reflects on 1) unlimited space, 2) unlimited consciousness, and 3) emptiness, and at the moments of the right attainments one relies on the other four aggregates, not on matter. As for the name of the fourth one: because identification is weak and because ignorance is namely superior, it is said to be 4) nonidentification. But it has weak identification and is said to be of no nonidentification. Such is the process: the sphere of unlimited space, the sphere of unlimited consciousness, the sphere of emptiness, and the sphere of neither identification nor nonidentification. These are the names of the four immaterial ones. If one adds the attainment of cessation, one also uses the term nine gradual spiritual attainments.[70]

The four immeasurables are benevolence (*maitrī*), compassion (*karuṇā*), sympathetic joy (*muditā*), and equanimity (*upekṣā*). The nature of the first two among the four is the absence of hatred. Sympathetic joy is the feeling of contentedness. Equanimity is the absence of attachment. Their objects are the sentient beings in the realm of desire. The malice and gladness, attachment, anger, and so on [of beings] are thus remedied.

The eight liberations depend on the first two [of the four] trances: 1) the liberation in which one inwardly has a notion of matter and contemplates external matter. The notion of its foulness becomes the notion of blue [of a corpse]. With matter one contemplates matter. 2) The liberation in which one inwardly has no notion of matter and one contemplates external matter. One contemplates without any internal matter. 3) The pure liberation based on the last trance. One dwells in its possession through personal realization and watches all matter becoming pure and bright. Such are three kinds, and the four immaterial attainments are the next four liberations. The attainment of the cessation of feeling and identification is the eighth liberation.

Relying on awareness of the summit of existence, the noble ones are wearied with coarse feelings and identification, and because of their tranquil meditative attainment they extinguish awareness and the accompanying mental factors. This is called attainment of cessation.

The ten all-bases: one totally contemplates earth, water, fire, wind, blue, yellow, red, white, and the two spheres of unlimited space and of unlimited consciousness. Depending on the fourth trance one totally and without interruption contemplates the earth base and and so on, taking the visible matter of [the realm of] desire as object. The first eight among the ten have the nature of absence of attachment. The last two are subsequently the immaterial ones of space and of consciousness by nature.

The eight spheres of mastery: 1) Inwardly having a notion of matter, one contemplates few external forms; 2) inwardly having a notion of matter, one contemplates many external forms; 3) inwardly without any notion of matter, one contemplates few external forms; 4) inwardly without any notion of matter, one contemplates many external forms; 5) inwardly without any notion of matter, one contemplates external forms, the four blue, yellow, red, and white. With the first ones they become eight. The first two among the eight are like the first liberation. The next two are like the next liberation. The last four are like the third liberation.

[*Question:*] What is the difference between such eight spheres of mastery and the three liberations?

Answer: The liberations that were previously developed can only reject. These spheres of mastery that are developed can control their object. At one's wish it will never arise. As for the goal of the development of liberations, and so on:[71] 1) delusions are abandoned and far removed, and 2) obtaining excellent sovereignty in concentration. One can therefore produce the qualities of dis-
236a passion and so on, and also the excellent higher faculties. Through these one can change anything. One may retain or abandon, because one brings about causes in various ways.

The three *samādhis* of emptiness, signlessness, and aimlessness. The *samādhi* of emptiness is a concentration associated with the two aspects: empty and selfless. The *samādhi* of signlessness is a concentration associated with the four aspects when taking the truth of cessation as its object.[72] Nirvana is signless, free from the ten signs (*nimitta*),[73] and so one uses the term signlessness. Taking that concentration as one's object, one obtains what is called signlessness. The *samādhi* of aimlessness takes the remaining ten aspects of the truths as its object, being a concentration that is associated with them: impermanent and painful, and the cause, because of their distress; the path because of the need to abandon, just like a raft.[74] Taking that concentration as one's object, one obtains the term aimlessness. This *samādhi* is in any case a passage as it addresses [the ten aspects].[75]

Because these qualities are common to the twice-liberated arhats (because one who is liberated through wisdom is without the three concentrations and the four immeasurables), *pratyeka-buddhas*, and Tathāgatas, they are called common qualities.[76]

There are eighteen unique factors (*āveṇikadharma*) of a Tathāgata: the ten powers (*bala*), the four confidences (*vaiśāradya*), the three establishments of mindfulness (*smṛtyupasthāna*), and one great compassion (*mahākaruṇā*).

The ten powers[77] are: 1) the power of the knowledge of the possible and of the impossible, 2) the power of the knowledge of the maturation of actions, 3) the power of the knowledge of the trances, liberations, concentrations, and attainments, 4) the power of the knowledge of the degree of the faculties [of beings], 5) the power of the knowledge of the various resolves [of beings], 6) the power of the knowledge of the various elements [of beings], 7) the power of the knowledge of the ways to every destination, 8) the power of the knowledge of previous existences, 9) the power of the knowledge of birth and death, and 10) the power of the knowledge of the destruction of impurities.

The four confidences[78] are: 1) the confidence of perfect enlightenment, 2) the confidence of the destruction of impurity, 3) the confidence of the explanation of obstacles, and 4) the confidence of the explanation of the path. Because one is not afraid of others, as one has the power of knowledge, they are called confidences.

As for the so-called three establishments of mindfulness,[79] when the Tathāgata expounds the doctrine and the disciples are wholly respectful and practice with the right feeling, and when the Tathāgata does not become happy because of this but maintains equanimity, with right mindfulness (*smṛti*) and with right knowledge (*saṃprajāna*), this is said to be the first establishment of mindfulness of a Tathāgata. When the assembly of disciples is not respectful and does not practice with the right feeling, and when the Tathāgata does not become aggrieved because of that but maintains equanimity, with right mindfulness and right knowledge, this is said to be the second establishment of mindfulness of a Tathāgata. When the assembly of disciples on one hand is respectful and practices with the right feeling but on the other hand is disrespectful and does not practice with the right feeling, and when the Tathāgata does not become either happy or aggrieved because of that but maintains equanimity, with right mindfulness and right knowledge, this is said to be the third establishment of mindfulness of a Tathāgata. Because these three all are mindfulness and wisdom by nature, they are called establishments of mindfulness.

236b Great compassion: during the six times in the period of day and night in every world, he contemplates who suffers and who is happy in the world, and who deserves training and consequent benefit. That is why it is called great compassion.

The eighteen unique factors of a Tathāgata and his three points that do not need to be guarded[80] are expounded in Mahayana, as the vehicle of the disciples (*śrāvaka*s) has never heard of them.[81]

V. The Unconditioned Factors

Furthermore, there are three unconditioned factors (*asaṃskṛta dharma*): space (*ākāśa*), calculated cessation (*pratisaṃkhyānirodha*), and uncalculated cessation (*apratisaṃkhyānirodha*).[82] 1) The unconditioned [factor of] space: space has only non-returning as its nature. Because it is everywhere unhindered, one uses the term the unconditioned [factor of] space. When matter proceeds there, everything else—doors, windows and openings, any light or darkness, the sky or *agha* (sky)-matter—all are not unconditioned. 2) The unconditioned [factor of] calculated cessation, that is, when pure knowledge does away with any obstructing taint. For the reality manifested by the two paths [of] vision and of mental practice, one uses the term unconditioned [factor of] calculated cessation. 3) The unconditioned [factor of] uncalculated cessation. When one can forever stop the future coming into existence of the factors, one obtains a cessation, called uncalculated cessation, that is different from the previous one. When one obtains [this cessation], not because of any calculation but because one lacks the circumstances, one uses the term uncalculated cessation.

As for these three unconditioned [factors], the Sarvāstivādins concede that they have substance, but Sautrāntika masters maintain that they are not formed.

Question: Why would suchness not be unconditioned?

Answer: It is selfless. The vehicle of the disciples does not assert that a factor is selfless. And so the selflessness of the individual is the sixteen aspects: impermanent, and so on. The aspects of the three truths are conditioned. The aspects of the truth of cessation are only the factor [of calculated] cessation, because they are nothing else. And so the inanimate and the animate worlds, the path, fruition, and the unconditioned [factors] are the five things that may be known, because they comprise all factors that may be known.

The factors of the animate and inanimate worlds are the truth of suffering. The cause that realizes them is the truth of origination. The two factors—of the path and of fruition—are the truth of the path. The unconditioned [factor of] calculated cessation is the truth of cessation. Space and uncalculated cessation are two kinds of unconditioned [factors]. The two kinds are not comprised by the four truths, because the two truths [of] suffering and origination are impure factors, and because the two truths [of] the path and cessation are pure factors. Thus the knowable factors, both mundane and supramundane, both conditioned and unconditioned, have been explained.

Afterword

1. At the frequent request of the noble, wealthy, and intelligent crown prince [Zhenjin], Blo-gros-rgyal-mtshan dPal-bzaṅ-po [Matidhvaja Śrībhadra]

2. has applied his mindfulness to the sun: the *Kośa-śāstra* (*Treatise on the Treasury*), giving rise to the Abhidharma in the world. Relying on it, he has composed this treatise on what should be known by beings.

3. The guidelines are endless but he has compiled an outline
236c in a series of five: the inanimate [world], the animate [world], the path, fruition, and the unconditioned factors.

4. And so they are clearly shown in detail now, in a lucid and clear explanation. Yes, having understood this [*Treatise on the*] *Elucidation of the Knowable,* one may further show it to others.

5. Phrases of this treatise may run counter to what is meaningful, my indolence being excessive, but I do wish for the patient forbearance of the wise and also of the one who requested it.

6. May the good roots that are produced extend on all sides in the realm of space. I wish to realize the unsurpassed fruition together with all beings.

The *Treatise on the Elucidation of the Knowable,* [written] at the request of the crown prince, Bodhisattva Zhenjin (Jiṅ-gim), compiled by the *bhikṣu* ’Phags-pa Matidhvaja Śrībhadra, who takes the dust upon his head of the feet of the Dharma King and Superior Master (lama) Sa-skya Mahāpaṇḍita in the year 1278,[83] on the third day of the last decade of the middle autumn month (September 12), a day under the constellation of Puṣya, at the great glorious Dharma seat of Sa-skya.

Recorded by Miaoyin (Ghoṣaka) and Zhishizi (Prajñāsiṃha), possessing the scriptural texts, the discipline, and the treatises.

Notes

1 The measurements in this passage follow these linear measurements:
Seven near-emptinesses = one particle, *paramāṇu.* "Near-emptiness" is often used as an old translation for *paramāṇu.*
Seven *paramāṇu* = one atom, *aṇu.*
Seven *aṇu* = one *loharajas,* gold atom.
Seven *loharajas* = one *abrajas,* water atom.
Seven *abrajas* = one *śaśarajas,* (width of the tip of a) hare's hair.
Seven *śaśarajas* = one *avirajas,* sheep's hair.
Seven *avirajas* = one *gorajas,* bullock's hair.
Seven *gorajas* = one *chidra,* (dust mote seen in ray of sunlight through a) fissure (in a wall), i.e., *vātāyanacchidrarajas.*
Seven *chidra* = one *likṣā,* nit.
Seven *likṣā* = one *yūka,* louse.
Seven *yūka* = one *yava,* barleycorn.
Seven *yava* = one *aṅguliparvan,* finger joint, i.e., the distance between two joints of a finger.
Three *parvan* = one *aṅguli,* inch, i.e., the width of a finger.
Twenty-four *aṅguli* = one *hasta,* cubit.
Four *hasta* = one *dhanus,* arc, i.e., bow-length.
Five hundred *dhanus* = one *krośa,* the distance of a cow's bellowing.
Eight *krośa* = one *yojana,* the distance an ox yoked to a cart could pull.

2 The picture is as follows: the wind circle is at the bottom; the water circle is formed on its surface. Above it is a golden-earth layer, which sustains Mount Sumeru in the middle. There are seven concentric golden mountains, from Yugaṃdhara to Nimiṃdhara; the outer mountain is Mount Cakravāḍa, which is made of iron. Between every two mountains is an ocean. The seventh, last ocean, surrounded by Mount Cakravāḍa, is salty and the four great continents rest on it. To the south is the continent of Jambudvīpa, roughly triangular in shape, with two smaller continents at its tip, Cāmara and Aparacāmara. To the east is the continent of Videha, shaped like a half-moon, with Deha and Videha as secondary continents. To the north is the continent of Kuru, which is square, with Kurava and Kaurava as secondary continents. To the west is Godānīya, which is round, with Śāṭhā and Uttaramantriṇa as secondary continents.

3 One *lakṣa* = one hundred thousand.

[4] The eight qualities of water mentioned here and below in the text are: 1) cool (*śītala*), 2) clear (*accha*), 3) light (*laghu*), 4) savory (*svādu*), 5) soft (*mṛdu*), 6) fragrant (*niṣpūtigandhika*), 7) does not hurt the throat (*kaṇṭha*), and 8) does not hurt the belly (*kukṣi*).

[5] Kailāsa?

[6] Lake Manasa, Mānasarovar?

[7] The Śītā River: the Tarim or Yarkand River, resurfacing as the Yellow River in China, as Xuanzang says.

[8] Tibetan: *Brag gSer-gyi* (golden, *suvarṇa*) *bya-skyibs* (a rock where birds take shelter, *prāgbhāra*). Chinese: *ta,* as in *tāla,* surface (of a rock)?

[9] The Upper Swat Valley in Pakistan.

[10] Siṃhaladvīpa: Sri Lanka; Suvarṇadvīpa: the name of this continent continues for the island of Sumatra; Candradvīpa: the Buckergunge District in East Bangladesh? See Constance Hoog, *Prince Jiṅ-gim's Textbook of Tibetan Buddhism* (Leiden: E. J. Brill, 1983), p. 84, note 17.

[11] This agrees with the Tibetan version; see Hoog, p. 20.

[12] The eight hot hells are: Saṃjīva, "reviving"; Kālasūtra, "black thread"; Saṃghāta, "ground down"; Raurava, "cries"; Mahāraurava, "great cries"; Tāpana, "burning"; Pratāpana, "great burning"; Avīci, "immediate."

[13] The term "intermediate *kalpa*" is used to distinguish an *antarakalpa,* the original, "small" *kalpa* or eon, from a great *kalpa* (*mahākalpa*) of eighty *kalpa*s. A *kalpa* is traditionally measured using various metaphors, for example, the time needed to wear away a great rock by wiping it with a piece of soft cotton from Kāśī once every hundred years. See Akira Sadakata, *Buddhist Cosmology: Philosophy and Origins* (Tokyo: Kōsei Publishing Co., 1997), p. 96.

[14] The four supplementary hells (*utsada*) are: 1) Kukkula or Kukūla, "heated by burning chaff"; 2) Kuṇapa, "excrement"; 3) Kṣuradhārā, "sharp blades," which is further threefold—Kṣuramārga, "razor road," Asipattravana, "forest of sword-leaves," and Ayaḥśālmalīvana, "forest with iron thorns"; and 4) Kṣārodakā Nadī, "ardent river," called Vaitaraṇī, "without ford."

[15] The eight cold hells are: 1) Arbuda, "blisters"; 2) Nirarbuda, "abscess-cracks"; 3), 4), and 5) are onomatopoeic terms: Aṭaṭa, Apapa, and Huhuva; 6) Bursting Open Like an Utpala (blue lotus) Flower; 7) Bursting Open Like a Red Lotus (*padma*); 8) Bursting Open Like a Very Red (or crimson) Lotus (*mahāpadma*).

[16] This is added in Nianchang's text, *Fozulidaitongzai* (*Annals of Buddha and the Patriarchs through the Successive Dynasties*), p. 487a7.

17 This passage should be added. See the Tibetan version, Hoog, p. 29; Nianchang, p. 487b5; and *Kośa* III, pp. 170–171.

18 Nianchang, p. 487c17.

19 Nianchang, p. 488a6.

20 Can be found in the *Mahāyānasūtrālaṃkāra*. See Hoog, p. 85, note 40. Chinese text in Taishō Vol. 31, No. 1604.

21 See pages 18–19 of this volume, 227c15–228a15 in the Taishō edition.

22 Twelve *māsa*s = one *saṃvatsara* (year); thirty *ahorātra*s (night-and-day) = one *māsa* (month); thirty *muhūrta*s = one *ahorātra* (twenty-four hours); thirty *lava*s = one *muhūrta* (forty-eight minutes); sixty *tatkṣaṇa*s = one *lava;* one hundred and twenty *kṣaṇa*s = one *tatkṣaṇa.*

23 I.e., the Southern dynasty, Nanzhao, in Yunnan (937–1253 C.E.), vanquished by Qubilai.

24 In present-day Ningxia, Northern Shaanxi, part of Gansu and Qinghai. Xixia, the country of Śes-rab dpal, was a dynasty of the Tanguts from 1038 to 1227, when it was vanquished by Čingis.

25 557–649 or 650 C.E.

26 742–804 C.E.

27 The three kinds of vows of a monk, which are to keep 1) the *prātimokṣa-saṃvara,* the code of discipline, 2) the bodhisattva precepts, and 3) the esoteric precepts.

28 1229–1243 C.E.

29 Reigned from 1260–1294 C.E.

30 1243–1286, Qubilai's eldest son and heir-apparent in 1273.

31 Sarvāstivādins here means Vaibhāṣikas, for example, Saṃghabhadra. Vasubandhu is a Sautrāntika. See *Kośa* III, p. 66, note 5.

32 These two paragraphs outline the categorization of the four truths: in progressive dependent origination, the truths of origination (*samudaya*) and of suffering (*duḥkha*) are distinguished. In retrogressive dependent origination, the truths of the path (*mārga*) and of cessation (*nirodha*) are distinguished.

33 A variant list of the good generally permeating factors (*kuśalamahābhūmika*) adds absence of delusion (*amoha*).

34 A variant list of the defiled generally permeating factors (*kleśamahābhūmika*) has the six less lethargy, but adding wrong attention (*ayoniśomanaskāra*), wrong resolve (*mithyādhimokṣa*), incorrect knowledge (*asaṃprajanya*), forgetfulness (*muṣitasmṛtitā*), and distraction (*vikṣepa*), for a total of ten.

35 The Vaibhāṣikas (Sarvāstivādins in the text here) say that the dissociated factors (*viprayukta*) are different from matter (*rūpa*), awareness (*citta*), and accompanying mental factors (*caitasika*). Sautrāntikas say that these three are not different from the dissociated factors.

36 The formation aggregate (*saṃskāraskandha*) consists of: 1) the forty-six accompanying mental factors (*caitasika*) minus the first two of the generally permeating mental factors (*mahābhūmika*), feeling (*vedanā*), and identification (*saṃjñā*); 2) the fourteen dissociated factors (*viprayukta*).

37 The ten elements (*dhātu*) of the material factors are the five sense faculties (*indriya*) of eye, ear, nose tongue, body, and mind and their five respective objects. The seven elements of the factor of awareness are the six consciousnesses and the mind faculty. These seven elements are the *āyatana* mind, *manas*. The accompanying mental factors (*caitasika*), the dissociated factors (*viprayukta*), the unconditioned factors (*asaṃskṛta*), and unmanifest matter (*avijñaptirūpa*) are collectively called the element factors (*dharmadhātu*), also the base factors (*dharmāyatana*).

38 I.e., *gotra*. For the relation of spiritual family with the six kinds of arhats, see *Kośa* VI, p. 252–3; see especially p. 252, note 4.

39 I.e., the path of accumulation, *saṃbhāramārga*. The four establishments of mindfulness (*smṛtyupasthāna*), are mentioned: 1) mindfulness of the body (*kāyasmṛtyupasthāna*), 2) mindfulness of feeling (*vedanāsmṛtyupasthāna*), 3) mindfulness of awareness (*cittasmṛtyupasthāna*), and 4) mindfulness of the factors (*dharmasmṛtyupasthāna*).

40 I.e., *prayogamārga*. In the path of preparatory application one follows the four wholesome roots, aids to penetration (*nirvedhabhāgīya kuśalamūla*): 1) heat (*uṣmagata*) and the four right exertions or abandonments (*samyakpradhāna* or *samyakprahāṇa*); 2) summit (*mūrdhan*) and the four bases of supernatural power (*ṛddhipāda*): concentration of interest in good factors (*chanda-samādhi*), concentration of the effort to rejoice in the good (*vīrya-samādhi*), concentration of attention to good awareness (*citta-samādhi*), and concentration of investigation into the good (*mīmāṃsa-samādhi*); 3) patient acceptance (*kṣānti*) and the five faculties: faith (*śraddhā*), energy (*vīrya*), mindfulness (*smṛti*), concentration (*samādhi*), and wisdom (*prajñā*); and 4) the highest worldly factor (*laukikāgradharma*) with the five powers (*bala*), i.e., faith, energy, mindfulness, concentration, and wisdom.

41 The noble eightfold path, the teaching of the fourth noble truth: 1) right view (*dṛṣṭi*), 2) right thought (*saṃkalpa*), 3) right speech (*vāc*), 4) right action (*karmānta*), 5) right livelihood (*ājīva*), 6) right effort (*vyāyāma*), 7) right mindfulness (*smṛti*), and 8) right concentration (*samādhi*).

42 The following passages give an explanation of the ninety-eight

defilements and how they are abandoned in each of the four truths. There are ten fundamental defilements: 1) attachment (*rāga*), 2) repugnance (*pratigha*), 3) pride (*māna*), 4) ignorance (*avidyā*), 5) perplexity (*vicikitsā*), 6) belief in a self (*satkāyadṛṣṭi*), 7) extreme view (*antagrāhadṛṣṭi*), 8) attachment to moral precepts and vows (*śīlavrataparāmarśa*), 9) adherence to particular views (*dṛṣṭiparāmarśa*), and 10) false view (*mithyādṛṣṭi*).

To be abandoned through the vision of the four noble truths (*darśanaheya*):

In the realm of desire (*kāmadhātu*):
- truth of suffering (*duḥkha*) = ten defilements
- truth of origination (*samudaya*) = seven (less three: belief in a self, extreme view, and attachment to moral precepts and vows)
- truth of cessation (*nirodha*) = seven (less three: belief in a self, extreme view, and attachment to moral precepts and vows)
- truth of the path (*mārga*) = eight (less two: belief in a self and extreme view)

—these add up to thirty-two;

In the realm of form (*rūpadhātu*):
- truth of suffering = nine (less repugnance; no repugnance in the realm of form)
- truth of origination = six (less three: belief in a self, extreme view, and attachment to moral precepts and vows)
- truth of cessation = six (less three: belief in a self, extreme view, and attachment to moral precepts and vows)
- truth of the path = seven (less two: belief in a self and extreme view)

— These add up to twenty-eight;

In the realm of non-form (*ārūpyadhātu*)
- truth of suffering = nine (less repugnance; no repugnance in the realm of non-form)
- truth of origination = six (less three: belief in a self, extreme view, and attachment to moral precepts and vows)
- truth of cessation = six (less three: belief in a self, extreme view, and attachment to moral precepts and vows)
- truth of the path = seven (less two: belief in a self and extreme view)

— These add up to twenty-eight;

Thirty-two + twenty-eight + twenty-eight = eighty-eight.

To be abandoned through the spiritual path (*bhāvanāmārga*):
- in the realm of desire = four, i.e., attachment, repugnance, pride, and ignorance
- in the realm of form = three, i.e., the above four less repugnance
- in the realm of non-form = three, the above four less repugnance

— These add up to ten, for a total of ninety-eight.

In addition, each defilement is ninefold: weak-weak, medium-weak, strong-weak; weak-medium, medium-medium, strong-medium; weak-strong, medium-strong, strong-strong.

So, thirty-six (the ninefold four defilements) + twenty-seven (the ninefold three defilements) in each of the four trances (*dhyāna*) = one hundred and eight + twenty-seven (the ninefold three defilements) in each of the four attainments (*samāpatti*) = one hundred and eight = two hundred and fifty-two.

43 In the spiritual path (*bhāvanāmārga*) one practices the seven factors of enlightenment (*saṃbodhyaṅga*): 1) mindfulness (*smṛti*), 2) wisdom (*prajñā*), investigation of factors (*dharmapravicaya*), 3) energy (*vīrya*), 4) joy (*prīti*), 5) tranquility (*praśrabdhi*), 6) equanimity (*upekṣā*), and 7) concentration (*samādhi*).

44 Should be pride (*māna*), not delusion (*moha*), which is synonymous with ignorance (*avidyā*). See Hoog, p. 64.

45 The text mistakenly has "one hundred and fifty-two" here, which has been corrected. See note 42 and Hoog, p. 64.

46 After the previous paths, commonly known as the path of the learner, (*śaikṣamārga*), follows the path of the adept (*aśaikṣamārga*). The adept (*aśaikṣa*) realizes ten factors: the noble eightfold path, from right view (*samyagdṛṣṭi*) to right concentration (*samyaksamādhi*), plus right liberation (*samyagvimukti*) and knowledge of right liberation (*samyagvimuktijñāna*). See *Kośa* VI, p. 295.

47 The thirty-seven factors of enlightenment (*bodhipākṣikadharma*) are: the four establishments of mindfulness (*smṛtyupasthāna*), the four right exertions (*samyakpradhāna*), the four bases of supernatural power (*ṛddhipāda*), the five faculties (*indriya*), the five powers (*bala*), the noble eightfold path (*āryamārga*), and the seven factors of enlightenment (*saṃbodhyaṅga*).

48 The four establishments of mindfulness, which contribute to liberation (*mokṣabhāgīya*) in the path of accumulation (*saṃbhāramārga*), and the four wholesome roots, which contribute to intellectual penetration (*nirvedhabhāgīya*) in the path of preparatory application (*prayogamārga*). See also notes 39 and 40.

49 The four fruitions of the path of the *śramaṇa* are: 1) fruition of the stream-enterer (*srotaāpattiphala*), 2) fruition of the once-returner (*sakṛdāgāmiphala*), 3) fruition of the non-returner (*anāgāmiphala*), and 4) fruition of arhatship (*arhattvaphala*).

50 Here the path of vision (*darśanamārga*) of the four truths is explained. One successively realizes the four truths in their four aspects (*ākāra*). For the knowledges (*jñāna*) associated with these, see notes 52, 53, 54, 55, and 56.

The sixteen aspects, i.e., the fourfold aspects of the four truths, are as follows. Suffering: impermanent (*anitya*), painful (*duḥkha*), empty (*śūnya*), and selfless (*anātmaka*). Origination: cause (*hetu*), origination (*samudaya*), source (*prabhava*), and condition (*pratyaya*). Cessation: cessation (*nirodha*), appeasement (*śānta*), excellent (*praṇīta*), and escape (*niḥsaraṇa*). Path: path (*mārga*), right (*nyāya*), mode (*pratipatti*), and leading to liberation (*nairyāṇika*). The sixteenth moment is the beginning of the spiritual path (*bhāvanāmārga*).

51 See *Kośa* VII, p. 78, for the three sufferings (*duḥkhatā*s), i.e., the suffering (*duḥkha*) *duḥkhatā,* the formation (*saṃskāra*) *duḥkhatā,* and the transformation (*pariṇāma*) *duḥkhatā.*

52 Of the four knowledges, two are in the realm of desire: 1) patient acceptance (of the knowledge) of the *dharma* concerning suffering (*duḥkhe dharma* [*jñāna*] *kṣānti*), and 2) knowledge of the *dharma* concerning suffering (*duḥkhe dharmajñāna*). In the two higher realms of form and non-form are the other two: 3) subsequent patient acceptance (of the knowledge) concerning suffering (*anvaya* [*jñāna*] *kṣānti*), and 4) subsequent knowledge concerning suffering (*anvayajñāna*).

53 This follows the same scheme as in note 52 above, with two in the realm of desire: 1) patient acceptance of the *dharma* concerning origination (*samudaye dharmakṣānti*) and 2) knowledge of the *dharma* concerning origination (*samudaye dharmajñāna*); and two in the higher realms: 3) subsequent patient acceptance concerning origination (*samudaye'nvayakṣānti*), and 4) subseqent knowledge concerning origination (*samudaye'nvayajñāna*).

54 Again, following the same scheme as in notes 52 and 53: 1) patient acceptance of the *dharma* concerning cessation (*nirodhe dharmakṣānti*); 2) knowledge of the *dharma* concerning cessation (*nirodhe dharmajñāna*); 3) subsequent patient acceptance concerning cessation (*nirodhe'nvayakṣānti*); and 4) subseqent knowledge concerning cessation (*nirodhe'nvayajñāna*).

55 See notes 52, 53, and 54 above.The fourth knowledge, subsequent knowledge concerning the path (*marge'nvayajñāna*) is no longer in the path of vision (*darśanamārga*) but in the spiritual path (*bhāvanāmārga*).

56 I.e., subsequent knowledge concerning the path (*marge'nvayajñāna*).

57 I.e., *bhavāgra,* the fourth and final stage in the realm of non-form, also called the base of neither identification nor nonidentification (*naivasaṃjñānāsaṃjñāyatana*).

58 The Prajñāpāramitā (Perfection of Wisdom) literature, for example Kumārajīva's *Pañcaviṃśatisāhasrikāprajñāpāramitā-sūtra*, Taishō Vol. 8, Number 223.

[59] The eight stages (*bhūmi*) are: 1) of bright vision (*śuklavidarśana*), 2) of the spiritual family (*gotra*), 3) of the eighth person (*aṣṭamaka*), 4) of vision (*darśana*), 5) of attenuation (*tanu*), 6) of nonattachment (*vīta-rāga*), 7) of skill (*kṛtāvi*)—attainment of this stage means arhatship for the disciple (*śrāvaka*), and 8) of the solitary enlightened one (*pratyekabuddha*), of which there are two types—like a unicorn, (*khaḍgaviṣāna*) and living with a group (*vargacārin*).

[60] Should be "once." See Hoog, p. 69.

[61] See note 47.

[62] The six perfections (*pāramitās*): 1) giving (*dāna*), 2) patience (*kśānti*), 3) morality (*śīla*), 4) energy (*vīrya*), 5) concentration (*samādhi*), and 6) wisdom (*prajñā*).

[63] The vehicle of the disciples (*śrāvakayāna*), i.e., the Hinayana.

[64] There is a giver, a recipient, and the act of giving.

[65] The ten bodhisattva stages (*bhūmi*): 1) of joy (*pramuditā-bhūmi*), 2) of purity (*vimalā-bhūmi*), 3) of radiance (*prabhākarī-bhūmi*), 4) blazing (*arciṣmatī-bhūmi*), 5) difficult to conquer (*sudurjayā-bhūmi*), 6) in view of wisdom (*abhimukhī-bhūmi*), 7) far-reaching (*dūraṃgamā-bhūmi*), 8) immovable (*acalā-bhūmi*), 9) of good thoughts (*sādhumatī-bhūmi*), and 10) of the Dharma cloud (*dharmameghā-bhūmi*).

[66] The four wisdoms of a Buddha: 1) great perfect mirrorlike wisdom (*ādarśa-jñāna*), 2) equality wisdom (*samatā-jñāna*), 3) discriminating wisdom (*pratyavekṣaṇā-jñāna*), and 4) duty-fulfillment wisdom (*kṛtyānuṣṭhāna-jñāna*).

[67] See note 46.

[68] I.e., the ten fundamental defilements (*kleśa*), see note 42; and the sixteen secondary defilements (*upakleśa*). See *Kośa* V, pp. 90–1.

[69] I.e., the summit of existence (*bhavāgra*). See note 57.

[70] I.e., the four trances (*dhyāna*), the four immaterial attainments (*ārūpya*), and the attainment of cessation (*nirodhasamāpatti*).

[71] See *Kośa* VIII, p. 210.

[72] All four aspects (*ākāra*) of the truth of cessation. See note 50.

[73] See *Kośa* VIII, p. 185. The ten signs (*nimitta*) are the five external bases (*āyatana*), the objects of the sense faculties, e.g., matter, etc.; the male and female marks; and the three characteristics of the conditioned: birth, duration, and death.

[74] The remaining ten aspects (*ākāra*) referred to here are: of suffering, the two aspects of impermanent (*anitya*) and painful (*duḥkha*); of cause, i.e., origination, all four: cause (*hetu*), origination (*samudaya*), source (*prabhava*), and condition (*pratyaya*); and of the path, all four: path

(*mārga*), right (*nyāya*), mode (*pratipatti*), and leading to liberation (*nairyāṇika*).

75 *Kośa* VIII, p. 186, note 3: *tadatikramābhimukhatvāt.*

76 All these qualities (*guṇa*) belong to the: 1) twice-liberated (*ubhayato-vimukta,* i.e., through the power of wisdom and concentration) arhat; 2) *pratyekabuddha,* and 3) Tathāgata.

77 See *Kośa* VIII, pp. 69–71.

78 See *Kośa* VII, p. 75.

79 See *Kośa* VII, p. 76.

80 I.e., *arakṣya.* Because the Tathāgata's conduct is pure, he does not need to guard his actions of body, speech, and mind.

81 The eighteen unique factors (*āveṇikadharma*) of a Tathāgata are explained in the *Kośa* VII, but the three points that do not need to be guarded (*arakṣya*) belong to the Mahayana.

82 See *Kośa* II, pp. 279 et seq.

83 The year Renyin is 1302, but Wuyin, 1278, is meant. See Hoog, p. 82. 'Phags-pa died in 1280. Zhenjin died in 1285.

Bibliography

Bagchi, P. C. "*Chang so che lun* (*Jñeya-prakāśa-śāstra*). An Abhidharma work of Śāskya-Paṇḍita of Tibet," in *Sino-Indian Studies,* Vol. II, 3–4, 1946–47, pp. 136–56.

Bareja-Starzyńska, Agata. "The Essentials of Buddhism in the *Čiqula kereglegči:* A Sixteenth-century Mongolian Buddhist Treatise," in *Studia Indologiczne,* Vol. IV, 1997, pp. 1–30.

Franke, Herbert. "Sha-lo-pa (1259–1314), A Tangut Buddhist Monk in Yüan China," in *Religion und Philosophie in Ostasien, Festschrift für Hans Steininger.* Gert Naundorf, Karl-Heinz Pohl, and Hans-Hermann Schmidt, eds. Würzburg, Germany: Köningshausen und Neumann, 1985, pp. 201–22.

Hoog, Constance. *Prince Jiṅ-gim's Textbook of Tibetan Buddhism.* Leiden, The Netherlands: E. J. Brill, 1983. Religious Texts and Translations Series: Nisaba Vol. 13.

La Vallée Poussin, Louis de. *L'Abhidharmakośa de Vasubandhu.* Six volumes. Brussels: *Mélanges Chinois et Bouddhiques,* Vol. XVI, 1971.

Sadakata, Akira. *Buddhist Cosmology: Philosophy and Origins.* Tokyo: Kōsei Publishing Co., 1997.

Willemen, Charles. "New Ideas about Sarvāstivāda Abhidharma," in the *Indian Journal of Buddhist Studies,* Vol. X, 1–2, 1998, pp. 82–94.

THE CYCLE OF THE FORMATION OF THE SCHISMATIC DOCTRINES

Contents

Translator's Introduction

The text translated here with the title *Cycle of the Formation of Schismatic Doctrines* (*Samayabhedoparacanacakra*) is number 2031 in volume 49 of the *Taishō Shinshū Daizōkyō*. Though brief, this text is of considerable interest to Buddhists and scholars of the history of Buddhism during its early centuries. The *Cycle of the Formation of Schismatic Doctrines* is an essay by the scholar-monk Vasumitra, concerning the unorthodox and schismatic doctrines within the Buddhist sangha (community of monks) that began to arise soon after the *parinirvāṇa* of the Buddha, and which led to the formation of a number of different schools. Vasumitra was looking back on this situation some four hundred years after the Buddha's passing. Thus, the text is an account, or record, of the proliferation of schools and the differing points of doctrines that separated them. It is both a history of early Buddhism and a lament for what had become of the Buddha's teaching.

Why did Śākyamuni's followers splinter into many contentious and wrangling groups? In some cases, certain monks remembered certain teachings of the Buddha differently than the versions preserved in the memories of other monks. This is not surprising given the fact that the teachings were passed down via oral tradition. The Dharma was not committed to written form until several hundred years after the Buddha's time. Consequently, there was variation in the memorized and orally transmitted material. Also, some parties within the sangha wanted a relaxation of some of the monastic rules, a move opposed by others. Other doctrines arose through the process of change in the conception of what constitutes a Buddha. As the view of the historical Buddha began to evolve and assume a more cosmic, universal nature, old doctrines had to give way to teachings that conformed to this new conception. These and other factors led to the development of new doctrines, and new schools arose out of this situation. This was the situation that Vasumitra refers to as a "disaster" in the *Cycle of the Formation of Schismatic Doctrines.*

This unsalutary state of affairs began, the author tells us, when a large number of monks began to promulgate doctrines that were abhorrent to the more conservative faction of the sangha. Each faction insisted that its version of the teaching was the correct one and no agreement was possible. Tradition has it that a council was called by King Aśoka (r. 268–232 B.C.E.) to settle the dispute but no reconciliation occurred, and the doctrinal schism became the basis for an actual schism in the sangha itself. The more conservative side, who were in the minority, began to call themselves the Sthaviras ("Elders"), while the larger group became known as the Mahāsāṃghikas ("Majority Party"). Thus, the Buddha-Dharma was divided into two, a division that has endured into modern times.

Many scholars interested in the history of Buddhism believe that the Mahāsāṃghika school may have been one of the primary sources for the ideas that were developed more fully in the later Mahayana tradition, which was to become the form of Buddhism prevalent in North and East Asia. Comparing the Mahāsāṃghika teachings listed by Vasumitra with the teachings of the Sthaviras, it is possible to detect a fundamentally different attitude toward such matters as the nature of a Buddha. Was Śākyamuni simply a human teacher, subject to the same law of impermanence as all living beings, or is a Buddha by nature a being of radically different order—if not completely divine, then very nearly so? Mahāsāṃghika teachings show the beginning of a process of elevating the historical Buddha to a much more exalted status.

The numerous sects that grew out of the original schism survived for awhile, taught their doctrines, and subsequently vanished. Almost none survived to today. Some had a strong effect on developments in later Buddhism, such as the possible roots of the Mahayana in Mahāsāṃghika doctrine. The Sarvāstivādins became famous for a type of literature called Abhidharma, which made careful definitions of terms found in the sutras, lists of relationships among the terms, and so on. The school itself did not survive, but the compendious *Abhidharmakośa* authored by the fourth-century scholar-monk Vasubandhu remained important for many Buddhists of later times. The school also left us their monastic regulations (Vinaya), important for comparative study. The Sthaviras migrated to Sri Lanka where they became known as the Theras ("Elders"). Their version of the Dharma spread to Southeast Asia, where it remains very influential in the modern-day cultures and societies of the region, including those of Thailand, Burma, Laos, Cambodia, and southern Vietnam. The Theravadin school, as it is now known, claims to teach the true, undistorted doctrines of Śākyamuni and rejects the teachings of the Mahayana traditions that perhaps got their start with the Mahāsāṃghikas centuries ago.

The reader will find here a number of doctrines that were very controversial in their day. The Vātsīputrīyas taught the real existence of the *pudgala,* "person" or "self." This is remarkable because all other sects of the time agreed that a fundamental teaching of the Buddha is that no inherently existing person, self, or being exists, and all modern forms of Buddhism likewise agree that no such entity exists. Yet, as we can see from this text, at one time this teaching was proffered by the Vātsīputrīyas in great seriousness. Other doctrines of a metaphysical nature indicate the great amount of speculation taking place in the Buddhist community after the *parinirvāṇa* of the Buddha. The number of these doctrines as well as their variety bear witness to Vasumitra's lament concerning the proliferation of novel doctrines and new schools.

Author of the Text

The *Cycle of the Formation of the Schismatic Doctrines* is attributed to a certain Vasumitra. The name Vasumitra recurs in many different traditions, standing among others for eight Sarvāstivādins, three bodhisattvas, three authors of the Avadāna literature, and so on. However, since these traditions were not independent from each other, the Vasumitras they refer to might have all been the same person.

Kuiji (632–682), author of a commentary on the Chinese translation of this treatise by Xuanzang (600–664), identifies the author of the *Samayabhedoparacanacakra* with the Vasumitra who lived about four hundred years after the Buddha's *parinirvāṇa.* Because this figure is said to have been one of the compilers of the *Abhidharma-mahāvibhāṣā,* we can conclude that he must have been a follower of the Sarvāstivādin school.

Texts and Translations

While the original Sanskrit text of the *Samayabhedoparacanacakra* has been lost, there are extant three Chinese translations and one Tibetan translation:

1. *Shibabulun,* Taishō Vol. 49, No. 2032, compiled by Kumārajīva in 401–413.

2. *Buzhiyilun,* Taishō Vol. 49, No. 2033, translated by Paramārtha in 548–569.

3. *Yibuzonglunlun,* Taishō Vol. 49, No. 2031, translated by Xuanzang in 662.

4. *Gshuṅ lugs kyi bye brag bkod paḥi ḥkhor lo,* Ōtani No. 5639, Tōhoku No. 4138, translated by Dharmākara and Bzaṅ-skyoṅ in the ninth century.

In addition, there are extant three versions of commentaries on the text:

1. *Bushiyilunsu,* by Paramārtha. Although the original text of this commentary has been lost, scattered fragments are found quoted in the *Sanrongengikenyūshū,* Taishō Vol. 70, No. 2300, written by Chōzen in 1208.

2. *Yibuzonglunlunshuji,* written by Kuiji in 662 (*Dainippon-zokuzō,* Vol. 3, fascicle 3).

3. *Ibushūrinronjukkimokuron* (*Subcommentary on the Yibuzonglunlunshuji*) by Eiten, 1791 (*Nippondaizōkyō,* part 3, Ronjobu, Shōchinchidoshūrinronshōsho).

4. *Ibushūrinronjukkihotsujin* (*Subcommentary on the Yibuzonglunlunshuji*) by Oyama Kenei, Kyoto 1891.

This English translation of the *Samayabhedoparacanacakra* is based on the seventh-century version by Xuanzang, the *Yibuzonglunlun (Ibushūrinron)*. The contents and structure of this text does not differ substantially from those of the other two Chinese versions by Kumārajīva and Paramārtha. In this translation I have omitted minor variants, while significantly different readings from the other two Chinese versions are provided in parentheses. Glosses, simple definitions, and the Sanskrit terms for certain words or phrases are also given in parentheses, while brackets indicate interpolated material to clarify meanings.

I wish to thank my student Dr. Paul Hoornaert, lecturer at Kanazawa University, with whom I read the *Yibuzonglunlun* in the seminar on Buddhist history at Tōhoku University during the academic years 1981–4, for his help in the preparation of this English translation.

THE CYCLE OF THE FORMATION OF THE SCHISMATIC DOCTRINES

by

Bodhisattva Vasumitra

Translated into Chinese by Xuanzang

Chapter I

Introductory Verse

When a hundred-odd years had elapsed 15a6
After the *parinirvāṇa* of the Buddha,
There arose [two] different schools of the sacred teaching.
This was the beginning of disaster.

As the clinging to divergent views kept on growing,
There accordingly arose many more [subsidiary] schools.
On the basis of their respective scriptures (Āgamas),
Each school asserted views that inspired the disgust [of other schools].

The great bodhisattva Vasumitra,
Endowed with eminent knowledge, intellect, and insight,
A great sage and Buddhist mendicant,
Looked back to those times and examined them critically.

Examining exhaustively all the various worldly views
That were whirling round and round,
And splitting apart the words of the Muni ("Sage," i.e., the Buddha),
He decided to expound all those teachings [in this work].

One should closely examine the teaching of the Buddha,
And, basing oneself on the teaching of the holy truths,
One should pick up the truth
As if gathering gold from heaps of sand.

Chapter II

Origin and Distribution of the Buddhist Schools

This is the tradition that was handed down to me from mouth to mouth: A hundred-odd years had passed since the Venerable Buddha entered *parinirvāṇa*. It was a far from saintly time, as if the sun had been setting for a long time.

At Kusumapura in the kingdom of Magadha, King Aśoka ruled over Jambudvīpa (India) under a white umbrella (i.e., a symbol of his sovereignty), his rule extending to gods and humans. During his reign the great Buddhist sangha was split for the first time.

In fact, because the four communities disagreed on their interpretation of the Five Propositions of Mahādeva, the Buddhist sangha divided into two schools: the Mahāsāṃghikas and the Sthaviras. The four communities were: 1) the Nāga community, 2) the barbarian community of the border region (Pratyantikas), 3) the community of the learned (Bahuśrutīyas), and 4) the community of the venerables (Sthaviras).

The Five Propositions are explained in the following verse:

> [Arhats] are tempted by others. [They still have] ignorance.
> They still doubt. They are made aware of their
> enlightenment by others (i.e., their teachers).
> The [holy] path is produced through the vocal expression
> [of suffering].
> This is the true teaching of the Buddha.

Later, during the second century [after the Buddha's *parinirvāṇa*], three schools issued from the Mahāsāṃghikas: 1) the Ekavyāvahārikas, 2) the Lokottaravādins, and 3) the Kukkuṭikas (Paramārtha: Kaukūlikas).

Subsequently, during the second century, still another school called the Bahuśrutīyas issued from the Mahāsāṃghikas.

And again during the second century, another school called
15b the Prajñaptivādins issued from the Mahāsāṃghikas.

At the close of the second century, there was a heretic mendicant who abandoned the heretical doctrine and converted to the Right Dharma. His name was also Mahādeva. He joined the Mahāsāṃghika order and received his final ordination (*upasaṃpadā*) in that same order. He was learned (*bahuśruta*) and diligent (*vīrya*). He dwelled on the Mountain of the Caitya (stupa), where he again discussed the Five Propositions in detail with the monks of his school. As a result of the ensuing controversy, the Mahāsāṃghika school split into three: 1) the Caityaśailas, 2) the Aparaśailas, and 3) the Uttaraśailas.

Thus there were four or five schisms in the Mahāsāṃghika school. The original school and its offshoots add up to the following nine schools: 1) the Mahāsāṃghikas, 2) the Ekavyāvahārikas, 3) the Lokottaravādins, 4) the Kukkuṭikas, 5) the Bahuśrutīyas, 6) the Prajñaptivādins, 7) the Caityaśailas, 8) the Aparaśailas, and 9) the Uttaraśailas.

The sangha of the Sthaviras maintained unity and perfect harmony for many years. At the beginning of the third century a minor controversy set in, as a result of which the sangha was divided into two schools: 1) the Sarvāstivādins, also called the Hetuvādins, and 2) the Pūrvasthaviras, who later changed their name to the Haimavatas.

Later, during the third century [after the Buddha's *parinirvāṇa*], a school called the Vātsīputrīyas issued from the Sarvāstivādins.

And again during the third century, four schools issued from the Vātsīputrīyas: 1) the Dharmottarīyas, 2) the Bhadrayāṇīyas, 3) the Saṃmatīyas, and 4) the Ṣāṇḍagirikas (Kumārajīva: Ṣaṇṇāgarikas).

Thereafter, during the third century, a school called the Mahīśāsakas issued from the Sarvāstivādins.

Later, during the third century, a school called the Dharmaguptakas issued from the Mahīśāsakas. The founder [Dharmagupta] held himself to be the successor of the master Maudgalyāyana.

At the end of the third century, a school called the Kāśyapīyas, or Suvarṣakas, issued from the Sarvāstivādins.

At the beginning of the fourth century still another school, called the Sautrāntikas, or Saṃkrāntikas, issued from the Sarvāstivādins. Its founder claimed that Ānanda had been his teacher.

Thus there were seven or eight schisms in the Sthavira school. The original schools and their offshoots total eleven schools: 1) the Sarvāstivādins, 2) the Haimavatas, 3) the Vātsīputrīyas, 4) the Dharmottarīyas, 5) the Bhadrayāṇīyas, 6) the Saṃmatīyas, 7) the Ṣāṇḍagirikas, 8) the Mahīśāsakas, 9) the Dharmaguptakas, 10) the Kāśyapīyas, and 11) the Sautrāntikas.

Of all the schools mentioned above I shall now explain the teachings originally held in common and the teachings developed later on which there was disagreement.

Chapter III

Doctrines of the Four Schools of the Mahāsāṃghikas

The propositions on which the Mahāsāṃghikas, Ekavyāvahārikas, Lokottaravādins, and Kukkuṭikas originally agreed are these:

1. All honorable Buddhas are beyond this world (*lokottara*).

2. All the Tathāgatas have no defiling (*sāsrava*) elements.

3. All words spoken by the Tathāgatas cause the wheel of the Dharma (*dharmacakra*) to turn.

4. The Buddha teaches all *dharma*s (Kumārajīva: all *dharma*s and all characteristics) in a single sound.

5. In what the World-honored One (Bhagavat) has preached, there is nothing untrue (*ayathārtha*).

6. The material body (*rūpakāya*) of the Tathāgata is truly limitless (*ananta*).

7. His supernatural powers (*prabhāva*) are also unlimited. 15c

8. The lifespan (*āyus*) of the Buddha is also beyond measure (*apramāṇa*).

9. The Buddha's [compassionate] heart never tires of awakening pure faith (*śraddhā*) in living beings in order to convert them.

10. The Buddha never sleeps nor dreams.

11. The Tathāgata answers questions [straightforwardly] without relying on reflection.

12. The Buddha never utters words, phrases, and so on, because he is always dwelling in contemplation (*samādhi*). But living beings rejoice, believing that the Buddha [really] utters words, phrases, and so on.

13. One instant of [the Buddha's] mind (*ekakṣaṇikacitta*) contains distinct knowledge of all *dharma*s.

14. [His] wisdom (*prajñā*), arising in unison with one instant of mind, understands all *dharma*s.

15. In the venerable Buddhas, the knowledge of cessation [of present passions] (*kṣayajñāna*) and the knowledge of no more birth [of future passions] (*anutpādajñāna*) operate uninterruptedly until they enter final nirvana.

16. When entering their mother's womb, bodhisattvas never pass through the embryonic stages of *kalala* (the embryo shortly after conception), *arbuda* (the fetus in the second half of the first month), *peśī* ("a lump of flesh"), or *ghana* (solid body). (Paramārtha adds: *śākhā, parāśākhā* [another limb of the body], *keśaromanakha* [hair on the head and body and the nails].)

17. When entering their mother's womb, all bodhisattvas assume the form of a white elephant.

18. All bodhisattvas leave their mother's womb from the right side.

19. No bodhisattva produces thoughts of desire (*kāmasaṃjñā*), anger (*vyāpāda*), or violence (*vihiṃsā*).

20. For the welfare of living beings, the bodhisattva is born in lower destinies (*durgati*) by the power of his vows (*praṇidhāna*) and is reborn there at will.

21. Through the knowledge following upon (*antikajñāna*) instantaneous clear comprehension (*abhisamaya*), one exhaustively comprehends all of the different aspects (*ākāra*) of the four truths.

22. The fivefold group of consciousnesses (*pañcavijñānakāya*), eye-consciousness, and so on, is accompanied by passion (*rāga*) and is free of passion (*virāga*).

23. The sixfold group of consciousnesses exists in the realm of form (*rūpadhātu*) as well as in the realm of non-form (*ārūpya-dhātu*).

24. The five material (*rūpin*) faculties (*indriya*) are [merely] lumps of flesh. The eye does not see forms; the ear does not hear sounds; the nose does not smell odors; the tongue does not taste flavors; the body does not feel tactile objects.

25. In the state of concentration (*samāhitāvasthāna*) one can utter words. In it the mind is sometimes disciplined, and sometimes inclined toward resistance.

26. One who has accomplished what is to be accomplished (*kṛtaṃ karaṇīyaṃ*) is free from clinging to *dharmas*. (Kumārajīva and Paramārtha: has no more *sthāna* [i.e., a place to stand or occur].)

27. The mind (*citta*) and mental activities (*caitasika dharma*) of the stream-enterer (*srota-āpanna*) are conscious of their own-nature (*svabhāva*).

28. Arhats also can be tempted by others (*paropahṛta*). They still have ignorance (*ajñāna*). They still doubt (*kāṅkṣā*). They are made aware of their enlightenment by others (*paravitīrṇa*). The path (*mārga*) is produced by the vocal expression [of suffering].

29. Suffering (*duḥkha*) can lead one to the path.

30. To say "Oh, suffering!" can be of help [in the production of the path].

31. Wisdom (*prajñā*) is a means toward the cessation of suffering and the obtainment of happiness (*sukha*).

32. Suffering is also a food (*āhāra*).

33. In the eighth stage (*aṣṭamakabhūmi,* the course of the *srota-āpanna:* the path of vision), one can also stay for a long time. From [the first aspiration for enlightenment (*bodhicitta*)] onward to (*yāvat*) the final stage of the impure path (*gotrabhūmidharma*), there remains the possibility of retrogression [from each stage].

34. A stream-enterer is still liable to retrogression, but an arhat is not.

35. There is neither mundane right view (*samyagdṛṣṭi*) nor mundane faculty of faith (*śraddhendriya*).

36. No morally indeterminate (*avyākṛta*) *dharma* exists.

37. One who has established himself in perfect conduct (*samyaktvaniyāma*) may be said to have eradicated bonds (*saṃyojana*).

38. Stream-enterers are liable to commit all sins, except the [five] grave sins (*ānantarya*).

39. All sutras preached by the Buddha are of explicit meaning (*nītārtha*).

40. There are nine unconditioned (*asaṃskṛta*) *dharma*s:

1) Cessation obtained through discriminative cognition (*pratisaṃkhyānirodha*).

2) Cesation due to absence of a productive cause (*apratisaṃkhyānirodha*).

3) Space (*ākāśa*).

4) The sphere of unlimited space (*ākāśānantyāyatana*).

5) The sphere of unlimited consciousness (*vijñānānantyāyatana*).

6) The sphere of emptiness (*ākiñcanyāyatana*).

7) The sphere of neither identification nor nonidentification (*naivasaṃjñānāsaṃjñāyatana*).

8) The own-nature of the members of dependent origination (*pratītyasamutpādāṅgasvabhāva*).

9) The own-nature of the members of the holy path (*āryamārgāṅgasvabhāva*).

41. The own-nature of the mind (*cittasvabhāva*) is originally pure (*mūlaviśuddha*). But when it becomes stained by the adventitious dust of defilements (*āgantukopakleśa*), it is said to be impure.

42. The latent states of defilements (*anuśaya,* dormant passions) are neither mind nor mental activities, and they have no object (*anālambana*).

43. The latent states of defilements differ from manifest defile-
16a ments (*paryavasthāna*) and vice versa, because the former do not arise in unity with mind, whereas the latter do.

44. Past and future have no substantial existence (*dravya*).

45. All *dharma*s (*dharmāyatana*) are not known by [mundane] knowledge (*jñeya*) nor apprehended by [a defiled (*sāsrava*)] consciousness (*vijñeya*). They can be directly realized [only by the arhat who has entered the path of vision (*darśanamārga*)].

46. There is absolutely no intermediate state of existence (*antarābhava*).

47. Stream-enterers also attain states of meditation (*dhyāna*).

Such are the teachings [originally] held in common [by the four schools of the Mahāsāṃghikas].

Chapter IV

The Later Differentiated Doctrines of the Four Schools of the Mahāsāṃghikas

The propositions that were developed later, on which the four schools did not agree, are:

1. To each separate aspect (*ākāra*) of the four truths there corresponds a separate comprehension (*abhisamaya*).

2. Some *dharmas* are self-made (*svayaṃkṛta*) (Paramārtha: suffering), some are made by others (*parakṛta*), some are made by both [self and others], and some are born in dependence on conditions (*pratītyasamutpanna*).

3 Two [different] consciousnesses can arise simultaneously.

4. The [*dharmas* of the] path (*mārga*) and defilements (*kleśa*) arise together.

5. Actions (*karman*) and their retribution (*vipāka*) exist simultaneously.

6. The seed (*bīja*) itself continues to exist in the sprout (*aṅkura*).

7. The great material constituents (*mahābhūta*) of the sense organs (*rūpendriya*) change (*pariṇāma*). The mind and mental activities do not.

8. The mind pervades the body (*kāya*) and, in accordance with its [sense organ] support (*āśraya*) and object (*viṣaya*), it contracts and expands.

These later doctrines underwent further development. New distinctions were made, resulting in an endless variety of doctrines.

Chapter V

Doctrines of the Bahuśrutīyas

The teachings on which the Bahuśrutīyas originally agreed are:

1. The following five utterances (*svara*) of the Buddha constitute his supramundane teaching (*lokottaraśāsana*), because they lead to the path of liberation (*nairyāṇikamārga*): 1) impermanence (*anityatā*), 2) suffering (*duḥkha*), 3) emptiness (*śūnyatā*), 4) no-self (*anātman*), and 5) nirvana is peace (*nirvāṇaśānta*).

All other utterances of the Tathāgata are his mundane teaching.

2. Arhats too can be tempted by others. They still have ignorance. They still doubt. They are made aware of their enlightenment by others. The path is produced through the vocal expression [of suffering].

Most of their other doctrines [of this school] are the same as those of the Sarvāstivādins.

Chapter VI

Doctrines of the Prajñaptivādins

The propositions upon which the Prajñaptivādins originally agreed are:

1. Suffering does not consist of the [five impure (*sāsrava*)] aggregates (*skandhas*).

2. The twelve sense fields (*āyatana*) do not really exist.

3. The cooperative formations (*saṃskāra*), which develop interdependently and form a harmonious continuum, are conventionally called "suffering." There is no [other] subject (*puruṣakartṛ*) of suffering.

4. Death is never untimely (*akālamaraṇa*). It is what one receives as a result of past actions (*pūrvakarman*).

5. Actions keep on growing and [finally] become a cause from which the fruition of retribution (*vipākaphala*) is born.

6. One enters the holy path (*āryamārga, anāsrava*) through the accumulation of merit (*puṇya*). There is no need for the cultivation (*bhāvanā*) [of knowledge].

7. The path, [once obtained,] cannot be lost.

Most of the other teachings [of this school] are the same as those of the Mahāsāṃghikas.

Chapter VII

Doctrines of the Three Schools of the Andhra Mahāsāṃghikas

The doctrines that the Caityaśailas, Aparaśailas (omitted in Kumārajīva and Paramārtha), and Uttaraśailas originally held in common are:

1. Many bodhisattvas are not [yet] free from [rebirth in] evil destinies (*durgati*).

2. The act of venerating (*pūjākara*) a stupa does not procure great fruition (*mahāphala*).

3. There are arhats who are tempted by others, and so on.

These propositions and most of the other teachings [of this school] are the same as those of the Mahāsāṃghikas.

Chapter VIII

Doctrines of the Sarvāstivādins

The propositions originally held in common by the Sarvāstivādins are:

1. According to the Sarvāstivādins, all things that exist are comprised in two [categories]: 1) name (*nāman*) and 2) form (*rūpa*). Past and future also have substantial existence.

2. All *dharmas* (*dharmāyatana*) are cognizable (*jñeya*), apprehendable (*vijñeya*), and comprehensible (*abhijñeya*).

3. The characteristics (*lakṣaṇa*) of birth (*jāti*), old age (*jarā*), duration (*sthiti*), and impermanence are not associated with the mind (*cittaviprayukta*). They are included in the group of cooperative formations (*saṃskāraskandha*).

4. There are three kinds of conditioned (*saṃskṛta*) and three kinds of unconditioned (*asaṃskṛta*) *dharmas*. The three characteristics of conditioned *dharmas* (*saṃskṛtalakṣaṇa*), [birth, change, and destruction,] each exist substantially (*dravya*). Three [of the 16b
four] truths, [suffering, its origination, and the path leading to its cessation,] are conditioned; one truth, [the cessation of suffering,] is unconditioned.

5. The four noble truths are comprehended (*abhisamaya*) gradually (*anupūrva*).

6. Based on the two meditations (*samādhi*) of emptiness and non-desire (*apraṇihita*), one can become established in righteous conduct (*samyaktvaniyāma*). Through meditating on desire, [the four aspects of the truth of suffering] (Paramārtha: things associated with the realm of desire), one can become established in righteous conduct. One who has already become established in righteous conduct is called "oriented" (*pratipanna*), while staying in the first fifteen moments [of the path of vision] and "abiding in the

fruition" (*phalasthita*) in the sixteenth moment (i.e., the first stage of the path of cultivation, *bhāvanāmārga*).

7. The highest worldly *dharma* (*laukikāgradharma*) is one [instant of] mind (*ekakṣaṇikacitta*). There are three kinds of highest worldly *dharmas*. (Kumārajīva and Paramārtha: There is retrogression from the other three members [i.e., the first three stages of the accumulation of good roots] of the preparatory path [*prayogamārga*].) There is absolutely no retrogression (*parihāṇi*) from the highest worldly *dharma*.

8. A stream-enterer does not retrogress [to a lower stage], but the arhat can retrogress [from arhatship].

9. Not all arhats attain the knowledge of no more birth [of future passions] (*anutpādajñāna*).

10. Even worldlings (*pṛthagjana*) can abandon desire (*kāma*) and anger (*vyāpāda*).

11. Even heretics (*tīrthika*) can obtain the five supernatural powers (*abhijñā*).

12. Some gods (*devas*) (those who dwell in the heaven of six desires) do observe chastity (*brahmacaryā*).

13. The [seven] factors of enlightenment can be obtained in the seven contemplations (*samāpatti*) (i.e., the four contemplations of the realm of form and the first three stages of the realm of non-form), but not in any other contemplation. All the meditations (*dhyāna*) are entirely comprised in the [four] abodes of mindfulness (*smṛtyupasthāna*). Without relying on [profound] meditation one can [not only] attain a steady abode in righteous conduct, [but] also attain arhatship (*arhattvaphala*).

14. As long as the body dwells in the realms of form (*rūpadhātu*) and non-form (*ārūpyadhātu*), one can attain a steady abode in righteous conduct but cannot attain arhatship. However, when the body resides in the realm of desire (*kāmadhātu*), one can not only attain a steady abode in righteous conduct but also arhatship.

15. In the northern continent of Kuru no one is free from passion (*virāga*). No arhat is born there nor among the unconscious gods (*asaṃjñideva*).

16. The four fruitions of religious life (*śrāmaṇyaphala*) are not necessarily attained gradually. One who has already attained a established abode in righteous conduct can, via the mundane path, obtain the state of once-returner (*sakṛdāgāmin,* the second stage of arhatship) and of non-returner (*anāgāmin,* the third stage of arhatship).

17. The four abodes of mindfulness (*smṛtyupasthāna*) may be said to include all *dharma*s.

18. All latent states of defilements (*anuśaya*) are mental activities (*caitasika*). They are associated with the mind and have an object (*sālambana*).

19. All the latent states of defilements are entirely comprised in the manifest defilements (*paryavasthāna*), but not vice versa.

20. The own-nature of the members of the chain of dependent origination (*pratītyasamutpādāṅgasvabhāva*) is definitely conditioned (*saṃskṛta*).

21. Some members of the chain of dependent origination function also in the arhat.

22. There is growth (*vardhana*) of meritorious actions (*puṇyakarman*) in the arhat.

23. The intermediate state of existence (*antarābhava*) exists only in the realm of desire and the realm of form.

24. The fivefold group of consciousnesses (*pañcavijñānakāya*), the eye-consciousness and so on, is [always] accompanied by passion (*sarāga*) and [is never] free from passion (*avirāga*). These [five] apprehend only the particulars (*svalakṣaṇa*) and do not conceive of the universals (*sāmānyalakṣaṇa*).

25. The mind and mental activities are substantially real (*dravya*). The mind and mental activities depend on objects (*sālambana*). No own-nature is born in unity with itself. The mind is not born in unity with the mind.

26. There is a mundane right view (*samyagdṛṣṭi*) and a mundane faculty of faith (*śraddhendriya*).

27. Morally indeterminate (*avyākṛta*) *dharma*s exist.

28. For arhats neither *dharma*s to be learned (*śaikṣadharma*s) nor *dharma*s not to be learned (*aśaikṣadharma*s) exist. All arhats obtain states of meditation; they can produce them but cannot gain clear comprehension (*abhisamaya*) of them. Some arhats receive the retribution of past actions.

29. There are worldlings who die in a good state of mind (*kuśalacitta*).

30. It is impossible that one's life ends while one's mind is in a state of concentration (*samāhitāvasthāna*).

31. The Buddha vehicle and the [other] two vehicles (i.e., that of the *pratyekabuddha* and that of the *śrāvaka*) do not differ as to the liberation (*vimukti*) [they lead to]. But the paths of the three vehicles [leading to liberation] do differ from each other. The benevolence (*maitrī*), compassion (*karuṇā*), and so on of the Buddha do not have living beings as their object. One who clings to the existence (*bhava*) of [the self (*ātman*) in] living beings cannot obtain liberation.

32. It should be said that bodhisattvas are still worldlings, because their bonds (*saṃyojana*) are not destroyed. If they have not yet become established in righteous conduct, they cannot be
16c said to have surpassed (*samatikrānta*) the stage (*bhūmi*) of worldlings.

33. "Living being" (*sattva*) is nothing but a name (*prajñaptimātra*), referring to the [physical and mental] continuum (*santati*) which is the object of attachment (*upādāna*).

34. It is said that all cooperative formations (*saṃskāra*) perish instantly.

35. There is absolutely nothing that transmigrates from a previous existence to a later existence. The *pudgala* (person), which transmigrates according to worldly people, is nothing other than various formations (*saṃskāra*) operative during a person's lifetime. At the time of nirvana without remainder (*anupadhiśeṣanirodha*), there are no more changing aggregates (*skandha*s).

36. There are supramundane meditations.

37. Examination (*vitarka*) [of the object of meditation] can also be undefiled. Good [actions] can be causes of rebirth.

38. In the state of concentration (*samāhitāvasthāna*) no words are uttered.

39. The noble eightfold path is the true wheel of the Dharma. Not all words of the Tathāgatas turn the wheel of the Dharma.

40. The Buddha cannot teach all *dharma*s in a single sound. Some sayings of the Bhagavat are not in conformity with truth (*ayathārtha*). Not all sutras preached by the Buddha are of explicit meaning (*nītārtha*). The Buddha himself has said that some sutras are not of explicit meaning.

These are the doctrines originally held in common by [all] Sarvāstivādins. The doctrines developed later on which they were in disagreement are innumerable.

Chapter IX

Doctrines of the Haimavatas

The fundamental propositions on which all Haimavatas originally agreed are:

1. Bodhisattvas are still worldlings.

2. Bodhisattvas do not enter their [mother's] wombs (*garbha*) out of attachment (*kāma*) [to life].

3. Heretics cannot obtain the five supernatural powers (*ṛddhi*).

4. None of the gods (*deva*s) (i.e., inhabitants of the heaven of six desires) observes chastity (*brahmacaryā*).

5. Some arhats are tempted by others. They still have ignorance. They still doubt. They are enlightened by others. The path is born by the vocal expression [of suffering].

Most of the other teachings [of this school] are the same as those of the Sarvāstivādins.

Chapter X

Doctrines of the Vātsīputrīyas and Their Four Schools

The propositions that the Vātsīputrīyas originally held in common are:

1. The *pudgala* (person) is neither identical to nor different from the aggregates (*skandhas*). "*Pudgala*" is a conventional designation (*prajñapti*) referring to the [five] aggregates, the [twelve] sense fields (*āyatana*), and the [eighteen] elements (*dhātu*). (Paramārtha adds: There are three kinds of *prajñapti*: 1] what comprises everything, 2] what comprises a part, and 3] what comprises liberation through cessation.)

2. Some formations (*saṃskāra*) endure for a while, and others perish instantly.

3. Apart from the *pudgala,* no *dharma*s transmigrate from a previous existence to the next one. The truth is that they transmigrate in dependence on the *pudgala* [with the *pudgala* as substrate].

4. Even heretics can obtain the five supernatural powers.

5. The five consciousnesses are neither accompanied by passion nor free from passion.

6. He who has destroyed the bonds (*saṃyojana*) of the realm of desire that are to be destroyed by [the path of] cultivation (*bhāvanāmārga*) is really free from attachment (*virāga*). However, one who has [only] destroyed the bonds that to be destroyed by [the path of] vision (*darśanamārga*) [is not really free from attachment].

7. It is said that establishment in righteous conduct can be obtained through [the stages of] patience (*kṣānti*), names (*nāman*),

aspects (*ākāra*), and the highest worldly *dharma* (*laukikāgra-dharma*). One who is already established in righteous conduct is called "oriented" (*pratipanna*) while staying in the first twelve moments of the path of vision and "abiding in the fruition" (*phalasthita*) while staying in the thirteenth moment.

(Paramārtha adds: 1] All living beings commit two kinds of mistakes: mistakes of the intellect [*manas*] and mistakes of fact [*vastu*?, i.e., natural, spontaneous mistakes?]; 2] the two main causes of samsara are defilements [*kleśa*] and actions [*karman*]; 3] two *dharma*s are supreme causes of liberation: meditative insight [*vipaśyanā*] and mental tranquility [*śamatha*]; 4] one who has sinned against the Right Dharma [*saddharma*] without his own-nature being the predominant condition [*adhipatipratyaya*] [of that sin] cannot be held responsible [for that sin]; 5] two things constantly operative in all living beings are the roots of defilements: wrong knowledge [*avidyā*] and the thirst for existence [*bhavatṛṣṇā*]; 6] there are seven pure abodes; 7] The Buddha's knowledge is dissociated [*viprayukta*] from the objects of moral conduct [*śīla*], and so on; 8] based on what has been clearly discerned, a comprehensive knowledge of all *dharma*s can be attained; 9] when cessation [*nirodha*] is included, there are altogether six; 10] in the realms of form and non-form no one attains establishment in righteous conduct; 11] bodhisattvas are always born in the middle; 12] one who has gained the knowledge of cessation [of present passions] [*kṣayajñāna*] and knowledge of no more birth [of future passions] [*anutpādajñāna*] may be called a Buddha; 13] the sutras preached by the Tathāgata have a threefold purpose: to show the demerits of samsara; to show the merits of liberation [*vimukti*], and not to show anything. Such are the major propositions [of the Vātsīputrīyas]).

When disagreement arose on the interpretation of a [certain] verse (*śloka*), [the Vātsīputrīyas] were divided into the following four schools: the Dharmottarīyas, the Bhadrayāṇīyas, the Saṃmatīyas, and the Ṣāṇḍagirikas. The verse in question is as follows:

Already delivered, one retrogresses again.
Retrogression is caused by desire.
One can return and reach the abode of calm and joy again.
According to desire one obtains supreme happiness.

Chapter XI

Doctrines of the Mahīśāsakas

The teachings originally held in common by the Mahīśāsakas are:

1. The past and the future do not exist. The present and the unconditioned (*asaṃskṛta*) exist.

2. There is simultaneous clear comprehension of the four noble truths. When realizing the truth of suffering, one can realize all of the [four] truths. One who has seen [the truths once in the path of vision (*darśanamārga*)] can see them [again and again in the path of cultivation (*bhāvanāmārga*)] in exactly the same way.

3. The latent defilements (*anuśaya*) are neither mind nor mental activities. They differ from actual, manifest defilements. The own-nature of latent defilements is dissociation from mind; the own-nature of manifest defilements is unity with mind. 17a

4. Worldlings cannot uproot desire and anger.

5. No heretic can attain the five supernatural powers.

6. None of the gods observes chastity.

7. An intermediate state of existence does not exist at all.

8. In the arhat there is no further growth of meritorious actions.

9. The five consciousnesses are accompanied by passion and are free from passion.

10. The six consciousnesses are all accompanied by attention (*vitarka*) and reflection (*vicāra*).

11. There also exists a *pudgala* who was born in the highest stage [of non-returner] (*anāgāmin*).

12. There is a mundane right view but no mundane faculty of faith.

13. There is neither supramundane meditation (*lokottara-dhyāna*) nor pure attention (*anāsravavitarka*) [and reflection (*vicāra*)].

14. Good [actions] are not causes of rebirth.

15. A stream-enterer is subject to retrogression [but] arhats are definitely without retrogression.

16. The [eight] members of the noble path are all included in the [four] abodes of mindfulness.

17. There are nine kinds of unconditioned *dharma*s:

1) Cessation obtained through discriminative cognition (*pratisaṃkhyānirodha*).

2) Cessation due to the absence of a productive cause (*apratisaṃkhyānirodha*).

3) Space (*ākāśa*).

4) The immovable (*āneñjya*).

5) The suchness of good *dharma*s (*kuśaladharmatathatā*).

6) The suchness of bad *dharma*s (*akuśaladharmatathatā*).

7) The suchness of [morally] indeterminate *dharma*s (*avyākṛtadharmatathatā*).

8) The suchness of the members of the [noble] path (*mārgāṅgatathatā*).

9) The suchness of [the members of] dependent origination (*pratītyasamutpādatathatā*).

18. Conception is the beginning, death is the end. All the great material constituents of the sense organs change (*pariṇāma*). The mind and all mental activities also change.

19. Because the Buddha lives in the sangha, giving (*dāna*) to the sangha procures great fruition but [great fruition is not attained] in particular [through] giving to the Buddha.

20. The Buddha [vehicle] and the [other] two vehicles (*yāna*) are one and the same path leading to one and the same deliverance.

21. It is taught that all formations (*saṃskāra*) perish instantly.

22. No *dharma* can transmigrate from a previous existence to the next existence.

Such are the teachings that [this school] originally held in common.

Chapter XII

The Later Differentiated Doctrines of the Mahīśāsakas

The doctrines developed later on which [the Mahīśāsakas] disagreed are:

1. The past and the future really exist.
2. The intermediate state of existence also exists.
3. All *dharmas* can be known and apprehended.
4. All actions (*karman*) are mental (*cetanā*). Actions of the body and of speech do not exist.
5. Attention (*vitarka*) and reflection (*vicāra*) arise together.
6. The big earth (*mahābhūmi*) lasts for one *kalpa* (i.e., a cycle of time comprising the birth, duration, and destruction of the world).
7. The act of making offerings to a stupa procures but little fruition.
8. The own-nature of latent defilements (*anuśaya*) is always present.
9. All aggregates, sense fields, and elements are also always present.

As to the doctrine of this school that developed later, divergent views arose because of different interpretations of the following verse:

> Five things definitely bind.
> From these all suffering is born.
> They are: ignorance, desire, passion,
> The five [false] views, and actions.

Chapter XIII

Doctrines of the Dharmaguptakas

The propositions originally held in common by the Dharmaguptakas are:

1. Although the Buddha is included in the sangha, giving separate gifts to the Buddha procures great fruition but giving to the sangha [does not]. The act of making offerings to a stupa procures great fruition.

2. The deliverance obtained by the Buddha [vehicle] and that obtained by the [other] two vehicles is the same but the noble paths [of each vehicle] are different.

3. Heretics cannot obtain the five supernatural powers.

4. The whole body of the arhat is pure (*anāsrava*).

Most of the other teachings [of this school] are the same as those of the Mahāsāṃghikas.

Chapter XIV

Doctrines of the Kāśyapīyas

The teachings originally held in common by the Kāśyapīyas are:

1. *Dharmas* (i.e., passions, *kleśas*), which are already destroyed (*prahīṇa*) and are known to have been destroyed (*parijñāta*), do not exist anymore. If not yet destroyed and not recognized as such, they continue to exist.

2. When the retribution of actions is exhausted, actions cease to exist. As long as they have not given their full retribution, they continue to exist.

3. It happens that formations (*saṃskāra*) are caused by the past but they are never caused by the future. 17b

4. All formations (*saṃskāra*) perish instantly.

5. The *dharmas* of the learners (*śaikṣa*) produce the fruition of retribution (*vipākaphala*).

Most of the other teachings [of this school] are the same as those of the Dharmaguptakas.

Chapter XV

Doctrines of the Sautrāntikas

The propositions on which the Sautrāntika school originally agreed are:

1. Because they taught that the aggregates (*skandhas*) transmigrate from a previous existence to the next existence, they were called "those who teach transmigration" (Saṃkrāntivādas).

2. Without following the noble path, definitive cessation of the aggregates cannot be obtained.

3. There are aggregates that have arisen from the root (*mūlāntaskandhas*). There are aggregates "of one taste" (*ekarasaskandhas* = *mūlaskandhas*).

4. In the state of worldlings there are also supramundane *dharmas*.

5. The *pudgala* as absolute reality exists.

Most of the other teachings [of this school] are the same as those of the Sarvāstivādins.

Chapter XVI

Concluding Verse

Having completed the translation of this treatise (*śāstra*), the Dharma Master (*dharmācārya*) of the Tripiṭaka (i.e., Xuanzang) summarizes the meaning of this new translation in a verse:

> After having examined many Sanskrit texts in detail,
> I translated the treatise on the *Cycle of the* [*Formation of the Schismatic*] *Doctrines* anew.
> As the text is satisfactory and its meaning free of error,
> The wise should zealously study it.

Bibliography

Bareau, André. "Trois traités sur les sectes bouddhiques, attribués à Vasumitra, Bhavya et Vinītadeva: Le cycle de la formation des schismes (*Samayabhedoparacanacakra*)." *Journal Asiatique* (1954): 229–66; (1956): 167–200.

Demiéville, Paul. "L'origine des sectes bouddhiques d'après Paramārtha." *Mélanges Chinois et Bouddhiques* 1 (1932): 15–64.

Kimura, Taiken, and Ryūsho Hikata. *Ibushūrinron.* In *Ronbu,* Vol. 13, *Kokuyaku Daizōkyō.* Kokumin bunko kankō kai edition. Tokyo, 1921.

Masuda, Jiryō. "Origin and Doctrines of Early Indian Buddhist Schools. A Translation of the Hsüan-tsang Version of Vasumitra's Treatise *I pu' tsung lun lun 'shu chi.* Translated with Annotations." *Asia Major* 2, fascicle 1 (1925): 1–78.

Teramoto, Enga, and Tomotsugu Hiramatsu. *Zōkanwa sanyaku taishō Ibushūrinron.* Kyōto, 1935.

Glossary

Abhidharma: A collection of treatises containing detailed analyses of the psychological and spiritual content of the early Buddhist teachings; one of the three divisions of the Tripiṭaka. *See also* Tripiṭaka.

Abhidharmakośa: A treatise on the Abhidharma by Vasubandhu, which reflects the transition from the Hinayana to Mahayana view and was important in the spread and development of Chinese Buddhism. *See also* Abhidharma; Vasubandhu.

adamantine (*vajra*): Diamondlike, indestructible; a term used in Esoteric Buddhism to describe the indestructible and pure qualities of something, i.e., adamantine teacher, adamantine seat, etc. *See also* Esoteric Buddhism.

Adamantine Vehicle (Vajrayana): A school of Buddhism that arose in India, developed from Mahayana teachings, and which spread into Tibet, China, and Japan from Central Asia and India along with the Mahayana. *See also* Esoteric Buddhism.

Āgamas: A body of scriptures containing the early teachings of the Buddha.

aggregate (*skandha*): The five constituent elements that form the illusory experience of individual existence, personality, or selfhood—1) form (*rūpa*), 2) feeling (*vedanā*), 3) identification (*saṃjñā*), 4) formation (*saṃskāra*), and 5) consciousness (*vijñāna*).

Ānanda: A cousin of the Buddha who was his close disciple and personal attendant.

arhat ("one who is worthy" of offerings): A saint who has completely eradicated the passions and attained liberation from the cycle of birth and death (samsara); arhatship is the highest of the four stages of spiritual attainment in the Hinayana. *See also* Hinayana; samsara.

asaṃkhyeya: "Incalculable"; a very high number.

Asaṅga: An Indian Buddhist monk (ca. fourth century C.E.); founder, with his brother Vasubandhu, of the Yogācāra school. *See also* Vasubandhu; Yogācāra.

Aśoka: King of the Maurya kingdom of northern India (r. 272–236 B.C.E.). A convert to Buddhism after a particularly bloody series of battles, Aśoka implemented a "reign of Dharma" and state support of Buddhism. According to the Sarvāstivādin tradition, during his reign the Buddhist sangha was divided by a schism that led to the development of two main schools; however, the chronicles of Sri Lanka ascribe the first schism to the reign of Kālāsoka of the Susunaga dynasty.

asura: A type of supernatural being, demigods that are constantly engaged in warring against other gods.

Avalokiteśvara ("Lord of Beholding"): The name of a great bodhisattva who represents great compassion. *See also* bodhisattva.

bodhi: Enlightenment; the state of the highest perfection of wisdom; the state of undefiled purity and eternal bliss.

bodhicitta: Aspiration for enlightenment.

bodhisattva ("enlightenment being"): One who has engendered the profound aspiration to achieve enlightenment (*bodhicitta*) on behalf of all sentient beings, through the practice of the six perfections (*pāramitā*s) and the eventual attainment of ten spiritual stages (*bhūmi*s). The spiritual ideal of the Mahayana. *See also bodhicitta;* Mahayana; six perfections; stage.

Buddha vehicle: The Mahayana teaching that enables all beings to attain Buddhahood. *See also* Mahayana; vehicle.

caitya. *See* stupa.

Chan (Japan, Zen): A major Mahayana school that teaches exclusive practice of meditation as its soteriological path; the word *chan* is a transliteration of the Sanskrit *dhyāna* (meditation).

dependent origination (*pratītyasamutpāda*): The basic Buddhist doctrine that all phenomena (*dharma*s) arise in relation to causes and conditions and in turn are the causes and conditions for the arising of other phenomena. Nothing exists independently of its causes and conditions.

deva: A type of supernatural being; a god, a divine being.

dharma: Any phenomenon, thing, element, or factor; the elements that make up the perceived phenomenal world.

Dharma: The truth, law; the teachings of the Buddha.

Dharma body (*dharmakāya*): One of the three bodies or manifestations of a Buddha, as ultimate reality or suchness. *See also* enjoyment body; transformation body.

Dharma-nature: The essential nature of all that exists; identical to suchness and the Dharma body. *See also* Dharma body; suchness.

dhyāna: Meditation; a state of meditative concentration and absorption; also sometimes referred to as a trance.

emptiness (*śūnyatā*): The absence of substantiality or inherent existence of the self and all phenomena (*dharma*s); all *dharma*s arise only through the dependent origination of causes and conditions (*pratītyasamutpāda*). Direct insight into emptiness is the attainment of *prajñā* (transcendental wisdom). *See also* dependent origination; *prajñā*.

enjoyment body (*saṃbhogakāya*): One of the three bodies or manifestations of a Buddha, a symbolic personification assumed by Buddhas both as a reward for the perfection of their practice and in order to expound the Dharma to bodhisattvas and others. *See also* Dharma body; transformation body.

enlightenment. *See bodhi.*

Esoteric Buddhism: A form of Buddhism that combines Mahayana teachings with ritual and meditative techniques explicated in texts called *tantra*s. Also referred to as Tantric Buddhism or Vajrayana ("Adamantine Vehicle") Buddhism. *See also* Adamantine Vehicle; Mahayana.

four great continents: According to Buddhist cosmology, the four large land masses of different shapes lying in the ocean around Mount Sumeru, each in one of the cardinal directions: 1) Videha to the east, 2) Jambudvīpa to the south, 3) Godānīya to the west, and 4) Kuru to the north.

Four Great Heavenly Kings: According to Buddhist cosmology, the guardian gods of the four directions, the kings of the four great continents surrounding Mount Sumeru: 1) Dhṛtarāṣṭra in the east, 2) Virūḍhaka in the south, 3) Virūpākṣa in the west, and 4) Vaiśravaṇa in the north. *See also* four great continents; Mount Sumeru.

four noble truths: The basic doctrine of Buddhism: 1) the truth of suffering, 2) the truth of the cause of suffering, 3) the truth of the cessation of suffering, and 4) the truth of the path, i.e., the noble eightfold path that leads to nirvana. *See also* noble eightfold path; nirvana.

gandharva: A type of superhuman being; a heavenly musician.

hell (*naraka*): The lowest state of samsaric existence, where those who have committed grave offenses are reborn and suffer torment for many eons. There are eight hot hells and eight cold hells. *See also* samsara.

Hinayana ("Lesser Vehicle"): A term applied by Mahayana Buddhists to various early schools of Buddhism whose primary soteriological aim is individual salvation. The four stages of spiritual attainment in the Hinayana path are that of stream-enterer, once-returner, non-returner, and arhat. *See also* arhat; Mahayana; non-returner; once-returner; stream-enterer.

hungry ghost (*preta*): Beings who suffer the torment of insatiable hunger.

kalpa: An eon, an immensely long period of time; also a period of great cosmic change.

Kośa. See Abhidharmakośa.

Kumārajīva: An Indian Buddhist monk-scholar and translator (344–413). He entered monkhood at seven and studied both the Mahayana and Hinayana in northwest India and elsewhere. Invited to China in 401, he translated numerous sutras and discourses, including the Prajñāpāramitā sutras. *See also* Hinayana; Mahayana; Prajñāpāramitā.

Mahayana: ("Great Vehicle"): A form of Buddhism that developed in India around 100 B.C.E. and which exalts as its religious ideal the bodhisattva, great beings who aspire to enlightenment on behalf of all sentient beings. The development of the Mahayana resulted in a great outpouring of Buddhist literature, including the Prajñāpāramitā sutras. *See also* bodhisattva; Prajñāpāramitā.

Maitreya: The future Buddha, currently still a bodhisattva. *See also* bodhisattva.

Mañjuśrī: The bodhisattva who represents wisdom. *See also* bodhisattva.

Māra: The personification of desire, death, the Evil One.

Mount Sumeru: In Buddhist cosmology, the highest mountain rising from the center of the world; it has four sides, is narrowest in the center, and is surrounded by eight mountain ranges; in the ocean between the seventh and eighth of these ranges are the four great continents inhabited by human beings. *See also* four great continents.

nāga: A type of supernatural being in the form of a dragon or serpent.

noble eightfold path: The eight aspects of practice for attaining nirvana, as taught by the Buddha in the fourth of the four noble truths: 1) right view, 2) right thought, 3) right speech, 4) right action, 5) right livelihood, 6) right effort, 7) right mindfulness, and 8) right meditation. *See also* four noble truths.

non-returner (*anāgāmin*): The third of the four stages of spiritual attainment in the Hinayana; one who has attained this stage is no longer subject to rebirth in the realm of desire. *See also* Hinayana; three realms.

nirvana: Liberation from samsara, a state in which all passions are extinguished and the highest wisdom attained; *bodhi,* enlightenment. *See also bodhi;* samsara.

once-returner (*sakṛdāgāmin*): The second of the four stages of spiritual attainment in the Hinayana; one who has attained this state is subject to rebirth only once in each of the three realms before attaining nirvana. *See also* Hinayana; nirvana; three realms.

pāramitā: See six perfections.

parinirvāṇa: Complete nirvana, commonly used to describe the death of the Buddha. *See also* nirvana.

passions: Mental functions that disturb and defile the mind and body. They are considered the cause of transmigration in samsara; by extinguishing them, one becomes an arhat. In the Mahayana, through recognizing the nonsubstantiality of the passions, a bodhisattva attains liberation and realizes *bodhi. See also* arhat; *bodhi;* bodhisattva; Mahayana; samsara.

prajñā: Nondiscriminating or transcendental wisdom; one of the six perfections. *See also* six perfections.

Prajñāpāramitā (Perfection of Wisdom): The name of a large body of important and influential Mahayana sutras expounding the doctrine of emptiness. *See also* emptiness; Mahayana.

pratyekabuddha ("solitary enlightened one"): One of the two kinds of Hinayana sages, along with *śrāvaka*s, who seek to reach the stage of arhat and attain nirvana. A *pratyekabuddha* attains liberation through direct observation and understanding of the principle of dependent origination without the guidance of a teacher, and does not teach others. *See also* arhat; dependent origination; Hinayana; nirvana; *śrāvaka.*

Sahā world: The world system that consists of Mount Sumeru at the center and the four great continents surrounding it, i.e., the world of human beings' existence. *See also* four great continents; Mount Sumeru.

Śākyamuni: The historical Buddha, who lived in India in the fifth century B.C.E. and whose life and teachings form the basis for Buddhism.

samādhi: A mental state of concentration, focusing the mind on one point; also a transcendent mental state attained by the repeated practice of concentration.

samsara: The cycle of existence, the continuous round of birth and death through which beings transmigrate; the world of suffering, contrasted with the bliss of nirvana. *See also* nirvana.

sense bases: The six objects of sensation and perception corresponding to the six sense organs: visual color and form, sound, odor, taste, tactile objects, and mental objects. *See also* sense consciousnesses; sense organs; sense perceptions.

sense consciousnesses: The consciousnesses that arise from the contact of each of the six sense organs with their respective objects—1) eye-consciousness, 2) ear-consciousness, 3) nose-consciousness, 4) tongue-consciousness, 5) body-consciousness, and 6) mind-consciousness. *See also* sense objects; sense organs.

sense faculties: The sense perceptions that correspond to the six sense organs—visual, auditory, olfactory, gustatory, tactile, and mental perceptions. *See also* sense bases; sense consciousnesses; sense organs.

sense fields: The six sense organs and their six corresponding objects. *See also* sense objects; sense organs.

sense objects: The objects of perception associated with each of the six sense organs—1) form (or matter), 2) sound, 3) smell, 4) taste, 5) tangible objects, and 6) mental objects. *See also* sense consciousnesses; sense organs.

sense organs: The six sense organs of the eyes, ears, nose, tongue, body, and mind. *See also* sense bases; sense consciousnesses; sense faculties.

six perfections (*pāramitās*): Six qualities to be perfected by bodhisattvas on their way to complete enlightenment—1) giving (*dāna*), 2) morality or moral conduct (*śīla*), 3) patience (*kṣānti*), 4) energy (*vīrya*), 5) meditation (*dhyāna*), and 6) wisdom (*prajñā*). *See also* bodhisattva.

śrāvaka: Lit., "word-hearer"; originally, a disciple of the Buddha, one of those who heard him expound the teachings directly; later, the term came to refer to one of the two kinds of Hinayana followers, along with *pratyekabuddhas*, to distinguish them from adherents of the Mahayana and Esoteric Buddhism. *See also* Esoteric Buddhism; Hinayana; Mahayana; *pratyekabuddha*.

stage (*bhūmi*): Ten stages of spiritual attainment accomplished by a bodhisattva on the way to perfect enlightenment. *See also* bodhisattva.

stream-enterer (*srota-āpanna*): The first of the four stages of spiritual attainment in the Hinayana; one who has entered the stream of the Dharma by destroying various wrong views. *See also* Hinayana.

stupa: A monument, usually in the form of a conical mound or structure, containing the relics of the Buddha or marking the site of an important event in the Buddha's life and which serves as a site for worship and veneration. Also called a *caitya*.

suchness: Ultimate reality; the state of things as they really are. Insight into the suchness of all phenomena, i.e., as empty of inherent self-existence, arising only through dependent origination, is perfect wisdom (*prajñā*). See also dependent origination; emptiness; *prajñā*.

sutra: A Buddhist scripture, a discourse of the Buddha. Capitalized, the term refers to one of the three divisions of the Tripiṭaka. *See also* Tripiṭaka.

Tathāgata: An epithet for a Buddha, meaning one who has gone to (*gata*) and come from (*āgata*) suchness (*tathā*), i.e., the embodiment of the truth of suchness. *See also* suchness.

three realms: The three classifications of samsaric states of existence: the realm of desire (*kāmadhātu*), i.e., the world of everyday consciousness accompanied by desires; the realm of form (*rūpadhātu*), in which desires have been eliminated but the physical body remains; and the realm of non-form (*ārūpyadhātu*), in which the physical body no longer exists. Each of these realms has various levels of heavens: six heavens of the realm of desire, seventeen heavens of the realm of form, and four heavens of the realm of non-form. *See also* samsara.

transformation body (*nirmāṇakāya*): One of the three bodies or manifestations of a Buddha, an incarnate physical body of a Buddha, such as Śākyamuni, that appears in the world in order to teach sentient beings. *See also* Dharma body; enjoyment body; Śākyamuni.

Tripiṭaka: The three divisions or "baskets" (*piṭakas*) of the Buddhist canon: the Sutras, discourses and teachings of the Buddha; the Vinaya, codes of monastic discipline; and the Abhidharma, treatises explaining the psychological and spiritual content of the Buddhist teaching.

universal monarch: A *cakravartin,* lit., "wheel-turning monarch," the ideal king as conceived of in Indian philosophy, said to possess seven treasures, including the wheel (*cakra*) that flies through the air and destroys his enemies.

Vasubandhu (ca. fourth-century C.E.?): Indian Buddhist monk, author of several important works, including the *Abhidharmakośa;* founder, with his brother Asaṅga, of the Yogācāra school. *See also Abhidharmakośa;* Asaṅga; Yogācāra.

vehicle (*yāna*): The various Buddhist paths of practice, suitable for the differing capacities of people. The Hinayana comprises the two vehicles of the *śrāvaka* and *pratyekabuddha,* contrasted with the bodhisattva vehicle of the Mahayana; these are collectively known as the three vehicles. The Mahayana concept of the One Vehicle incorporates all three vehicles in the one Buddha vehicle in which all beings may ultimately attain Buddhahood. *See also* Buddha vehicle; Hinayana; Mahayana; *pratyekabuddha; śrāvaka.*

Vinaya: Precepts and rules of conduct for monastics; along with the Abhidharma and the Sutras, one of the three divisions of the Tripiṭaka. *See also* Tripiṭaka.

yakṣa: A type of supernatural being; a kind of demon, fearsome in appearance.

Yogācāra: A major philosophical school of Mahayana Buddhism, founded by Asaṅga and Vasubandhu, ca. fourth–fifth centuries C.E., which advocates the doctrine of "mind-only" (*vijñapti-mātra*). *See also* Asaṅga; Mahayana; Vasubandhu.

Index

N

O

P

Q

R

W

A List of the Volumes of the BDK English Tripiṭaka (First Series)

Abbreviations

Ch.: Chinese
Skt.: Sanskrit
Jp.: Japanese
Eng.: Published title
T.: Taishō Tripiṭaka

Vol. No.		Title	*T.* No.
1, 2	*Ch.*	Ch'ang-a-han-ching (長阿含經)	1
	Skt.	Dīrghāgama	
3–8	*Ch.*	Chung-a-han-ching (中阿含經)	26
	Skt.	Madhyamāgama	
9-I	*Ch.*	Ta-ch'eng-pên-shêng-hsin-ti-kuan-ching (大乘本生心地觀經)	159
9-II	*Ch.*	Fo-so-hsing-tsan (佛所行讃)	192
	Skt.	Buddhacarita	
10-I	*Ch.*	Tsa-pao-ts'ang-ching (雜寶藏經)	203
	Eng.	The Storehouse of Sundry Valuables	
10-II	*Ch.*	Fa-chü-p'i-yü-ching (法句譬喩經)	211
	Eng.	The Scriptural Text: Verses of the Doctrine, with Parables	
11-I	*Ch.*	Hsiao-p'in-pan-jo-po-lo-mi-ching (小品般若波羅蜜經)	227
	Skt.	Aṣṭasāhasrikā-prajñāpāramitā-sūtra	
11-II	*Ch.*	Chin-kang-pan-jo-po-lo-mi-ching (金剛般若波羅蜜經)	235
	Skt.	Vajracchedikā-prajñāpāramitā-sūtra	

Vol. No.		Title	*T.* No.
11-III	*Ch.*	Jên-wang-pan-jo-po-lo-mi-ching (仁王般若波羅蜜經)	245
	Skt.	Kāruṇikārājā-prajñāpāramitā-sūtra (?)	
11-IV	*Ch.*	Pan-jo-po-lo-mi-to-hsing-ching (般若波羅蜜多心經)	251
	Skt.	Prajñāpāramitāhṛdaya-sūtra	
12-I	*Ch.*	Ta-lo-chin-kang-pu-k'ung-chên-shih-san-mo-yeh-ching (大樂金剛不空眞實三麼耶經)	243
	Skt.	Adhyardhaśatikā-prajñāpāramitā-sūtra	
12-II	*Ch.*	Wu-liang-shou-ching (無量壽經)	360
	Skt.	Sukhāvatīvyūha	
	Eng.	The Larger Sutra on Amitāyus (In The Three Pure Land Sutras)	
12-III	*Ch.*	Kuan-wu-liang-shou-fo-ching (觀無量壽佛經)	365
	Skt.	Amitāyurdhyāna-sūtra	
	Eng.	The Sutra on Contemplation of Amitāyus (In The Three Pure Land Sutras)	
12-IV	*Ch.*	A-mi-t'o-ching (阿彌陀經)	366
	Skt.	Sukhāvatīvyūha	
	Eng.	The Smaller Sutra on Amitāyus (In The Three Pure Land Sutras)	
12-V	*Ch.*	Ti-ts'ang-p'u-sa-pên-yüan-ching (地藏菩薩本願經)	412
	Skt.	Kṣitigarbhapraṇidhāna-sūtra (?)	
12-VI	*Ch.*	Yao-shih-liu-li-kuang-ju-lai-pên-yüan-kung-tê-ching (藥師琉璃光如來本願功德經)	450
	Skt.	Bhaiṣajyaguruvaiḍūryaprabhāsapūrva-praṇidhānaviśeṣavistara	
12-VII	*Ch.*	Mi-lê-hsia-shêng-ch'êng-fo-ching (彌勒下生成佛經)	454
	Skt.	Maitreyavyākaraṇa (?)	
12-VIII	*Ch.*	Wên-shu-shih-li-wên-ching (文殊師利問經)	468
	Skt.	Mañjuśrīparipṛcchā (?)	
13-I	*Ch.*	Miao-fa-lien-hua-ching (妙法蓮華經)	262
	Skt.	Saddharmapuṇḍarīka-sūtra	
	Eng.	The Lotus Sutra	
13-II	*Ch.*	Wu-liang-i-ching (無量義經)	276

Vol. No.		Title	*T.* No.
13-III	*Ch.*	Kuan-p'u-hsien-p'u-sa-hsing-fa-ching (觀普賢菩薩行法經)	277
14–19	*Ch.*	Ta-fang-kuang-fo-hua-yen-ching (大方廣佛華嚴經)	278
	Skt.	Avataṃsaka-sūtra	
20-I	*Ch.*	Shêng-man-shih-tzŭ-hou-i-ch'eng-ta-fang-pien-fang-kuang-ching (勝鬘師子吼一乘大方便方廣經)	353
	Skt.	Śrīmālādevīsiṃhanāda-sūtra	
20-II	*Ch.*	Chin-kuang-ming-tsui-shêng-wang-ching (金光明最勝王經)	665
	Skt.	Suvarṇaprabhāsa-sūtra	
21–24	*Ch.*	Ta-pan-nieh-p'an-ching (大般涅槃經)	374
	Skt.	Mahāparinirvāṇa-sūtra	
25-I	*Ch.*	Fo-ch'ui-pan-nieh-p'an-liao-shuo-chiao-chieh-ching (佛垂般涅槃略說教誡經)	389
25-II	*Ch.*	Pan-chou-san-mei-ching (般舟三昧經)	418
	Skt.	Pratyutpannabuddhasammukhāvasthitasamādhi-sūtra	
	Eng.	The Pratyutpanna Samādhi Sutra	
25-III	*Ch.*	Shou-lêng-yen-san-mei-ching (首楞嚴三昧經)	642
	Skt.	Śūraṅgamasamādhi-sūtra	
	Eng.	The Śūraṅgama Samādhi Sutra	
25-IV	*Ch.*	Chieh-shên-mi-ching (解深密經)	676
	Skt.	Saṃdhinirmocana-sūtra	
	Eng.	The Scripture on the Explication of Underlying Meaning	
25-V	*Ch.*	Yü-lan-p'ên-ching (盂蘭盆經)	685
	Skt.	Ullambana-sūtra (?)	
25-VI	*Ch.*	Ssŭ-shih-êrh-chang-ching (四十二章經)	784
26-I	*Ch.*	Wei-mo-chieh-so-shuo-ching (維摩詰所說經)	475
	Skt.	Vimalakīrtinirdeśa-sūtra	
26-II	*Ch.*	Yüeh-shang-nü-ching (月上女經)	480
	Skt.	Candrottarādārikāparipṛcchā	

Vol. No.		Title	*T.* No.
26-III	*Ch.*	Tso-ch'an-san-mei-ching (坐禪三昧經)	614
26-IV	*Ch.*	Ta-mo-to-lo-ch'an-ching (達磨多羅禪經)	618
	Skt.	Yogācārabhūmi-sūtra (?)	
27	*Ch.*	Yüeh-têng-san-mei-ching (月燈三昧經)	639
	Skt.	Samādhirājacandrapradīpa-sūtra	
28	*Ch.*	Ju-lêng-ch'ieh-ching (入楞伽經)	671
	Skt.	Laṅkāvatāra-sūtra	
29-I	*Ch.*	Ta-fang-kuang-yüan-chio-hsiu-to-lo-liao-i-ching (大方廣圓覺修多羅了義經)	842
29-II	*Ch.*	Su-hsi-ti-chieh-lo-ching (蘇悉地羯囉經)	893
	Skt.	Susiddhikaramahātantrasādhanopāyika-paṭala	
	Eng.	The Susiddhikara Sutra (In Two Esoteric Sutras)	
29-III	*Ch.*	Mo-têng-ch'ieh-ching (摩登伽經)	1300
	Skt.	Mātaṅgī-sūtra (?)	
30-I	*Ch.*	Ta-p'i-lu-chê-na-chêng-fo-shên-pien-chia-ch'ih-ching (大毘盧遮那成佛神變加持經)	848
	Skt.	Mahāvairocanābhisambodhivikurvitādhiṣṭhāna-vaipulyasūtrendrarāja-nāma-dharmaparyāya	
30-II	*Ch.*	Ching-kang-ting-i-ch'ieh-ju-lai-chên-shih-shê-ta-ch'eng-hsien-chêng-ta-chiao-wang-ching (金剛頂一切如來眞實攝大乘現證大教王經)	865
	Skt.	Sarvatathāgatatattvasaṃgrahamahāyānābhi-samayamahākalparāja	
	Eng.	The Adamantine Pinnacle Sutra (In Two Esoteric Sutras)	
31–35	*Ch.*	Mo-ho-sêng-ch'i-lü (摩訶僧祇律)	1425
	Skt.	Mahāsāṃghika-vinaya (?)	
36–42	*Ch.*	Ssŭ-fên-lü (四分律)	1428
	Skt.	Dharmaguptaka-vinaya (?)	
43, 44	*Ch.*	Shan-chien-lü-p'i-p'o-sha (善見律毘婆沙)	1462
	Pāli	Samantapāsādikā	
45-I	*Ch.*	Fan-wang-ching (梵網經)	1484
	Skt.	Brahmajāla-sūtra (?)	

Vol. No.	Title	*T.* No.
45-II	*Ch.* Yu-p'o-sai-chieh-ching (優婆塞戒經) *Skt.* Upāsakaśīla-sūtra (?) *Eng.* The Sutra on Upāsaka Precepts	1488
46-I	*Ch.* Miao-fa-lien-hua-ching-yu-po-t'i-shê (妙法蓮華經憂波提舍) *Skt.* Saddharmapuṇḍarīka-upadeśa	1519
46-II	*Ch.* Fo-ti-ching-lun (佛地經論) *Skt.* Buddhabhūmisūtra-śāstra (?) *Eng.* The Interpretation of the Buddha Land	1530
46-III	*Ch.* Shê-ta-ch'eng-lun (攝大乘論) *Skt.* Mahāyānasaṃgraha *Eng.* The Summary of the Great Vehicle	1593
47	*Ch.* Shih-chu-p'i-p'o-sha-lun (十住毘婆沙論) *Skt.* Daśabhūmika-vibhāṣā (?)	1521
48, 49	*Ch.* A-p'i-ta-mo-chü-shê-lun (阿毘達磨俱舍論) *Skt.* Abhidharmakośa-bhāṣya	1558
50–59	*Ch.* Yü-ch'ieh-shih-ti-lun (瑜伽師地論) *Skt.* Yogācārabhūmi	1579
60-I	*Ch.* Ch'êng-wei-shih-lun (成唯識論) *Eng.* Demonstration of Consciousness Only (In Three Texts on Consciousness Only)	1585
60-II	*Ch.* Wei-shih-san-shih-lun-sung (唯識三十論頌) *Skt.* Triṃśikā *Eng.* The Thirty Verses on Consciousness Only (In Three Texts on Consciousness Only)	1586
60-III	*Ch.* Wei-shih-êrh-shih-lun (唯識二十論) *Skt.* Viṃśatikā *Eng.* The Treatise in Twenty Verses on Consciousness Only (In Three Texts on Consciousness Only)	1590
61-I	*Ch.* Chung-lun (中論) *Skt.* Madhyamaka-śāstra	1564
61-II	*Ch.* Pien-chung-pien-lun (辯中邊論) *Skt.* Madhyāntavibhāga	1600

Vol. No.		Title	T. No.
61-III	*Ch.*	Ta-ch'eng-ch'êng-yeh-lun （大乘成業論）	1609
	Skt.	Karmasiddhiprakaraṇa	
61-IV	*Ch.*	Yin-ming-ju-chêng-li-lun （因明入正理論）	1630
	Skt.	Nyāyapraveśa	
61-V	*Ch.*	Chin-kang-chên-lun （金剛針論）	1642
	Skt.	Vajrasūcī	
61-VI	*Ch.*	Chang-so-chih-lun （彰所知論）	1645
	Eng.	The Treatise on the Elucidation of the Knowable	
62	*Ch.*	Ta-ch'eng-chuang-yen-ching-lun （大乘莊嚴經論）	1604
	Skt.	Mahāyānasūtrālaṃkāra	
63-I	*Ch.*	Chiu-ching-i-ch'eng-pao-hsing-lun （究竟一乘寶性論）	1611
	Skt.	Ratnagotravibhāgamahāyānottaratantra-śāstra	
63-II	*Ch.*	P'u-t'i-hsing-ching （菩提行經）	1662
	Skt.	Bodhicaryāvatāra	
63-III	*Ch.*	Chin-kang-ting-yü-ch'ieh-chung-fa-a-nou-to-lo-san-miao-san-p'u-t'i-hsin-lun （金剛頂瑜伽中發阿耨多羅三藐三菩提心論）	1665
63-IV	*Ch.*	Ta-ch'eng-ch'i-hsin-lun （大乘起信論）	1666
	Skt.	Mahāyānaśraddhotpāda-śāstra (?)	
63-V	*Ch.*	Na-hsien-pi-ch'iu-ching （那先比丘經）	1670
	Pāli	Milindapañhā	
64	*Ch.*	Ta-ch'eng-chi-p'u-sa-hsüeh-lun （大乘集菩薩學論）	1636
	Skt.	Śikṣāsamuccaya	
65	*Ch.*	Shih-mo-ho-yen-lun （釋摩訶衍論）	1688
66-I	*Ch.*	Pan-jo-po-lo-mi-to-hsin-ching-yu-tsan （般若波羅蜜多心經幽賛）	1710
	Eng.	A Comprehensive Commentary on the Heart Sutra (Prajñāpāramitā-hṛdaya-sūtra)	
66-II	*Ch.*	Kuan-wu-liang-shou-fo-ching-shu （觀無量壽佛經疏）	1753
66-III	*Ch.*	San-lun-hsüan-i （三論玄義）	1852

Vol. No.		Title	*T.* No.
66-IV	*Ch.*	Chao-lun (肇論)	1858
67, 68	*Ch.*	Miao-fa-lien-hua-ching-hsüan-i (妙法蓮華經玄義)	1716
69	*Ch.*	Ta-ch'eng-hsüan-lun (大乘玄論)	1853
70-I	*Ch.*	Hua-yen-i-ch'eng-chiao-i-fên-ch'i-chang (華嚴一乘教義分齊章)	1866
70-II	*Ch.*	Yüan-jên-lun (原人論)	1886
70-III	*Ch.*	Hsiu-hsi-chih-kuan-tso-ch'an-fa-yao (修習止觀坐禪法要)	1915
70-IV	*Ch.*	T'ien-t'ai-ssŭ-chiao-i (天台四教儀)	1931
71, 72	*Ch.*	Mo-ho-chih-kuan (摩訶止觀)	1911
73-I	*Ch.*	Kuo-ch'ing-pai-lu (國清百録)	1934
73-II	*Ch.*	Liu-tsu-ta-shih-fa-pao-t'an-ching (六祖大師法寶壇經)	2008
	Eng.	The Platform Sutra of the Sixth Patriarch	
73-III	*Ch.*	Huang-po-shan-tuan-chi-ch'an-shih-ch'uan-hsin-fa-yao (黄檗山斷際禪師傳心法要)	2012A
73-IV	*Ch.*	Yung-chia-chêng-tao-ko (永嘉證道歌)	2014
74-I	*Ch.*	Chên-chou-lin-chi-hui-chao-ch'an-shih-wu-lu (鎭州臨濟慧照禪師語録)	1985
	Eng.	The Recorded Sayings of Linji (In Three Chan Classics)	
74-II	*Ch.*	Wu-mên-kuan (無門關)	2005
	Eng.	Wumen's Gate (In Three Chan Classics)	
74-III	*Ch.*	Hsin-hsin-ming (信心銘)	2010
	Eng.	The Faith-Mind Maxim (In Three Chan Classics)	
74-IV	*Ch.*	Ch'ih-hsiu-pai-chang-ch'ing-kuei (勅修百丈清規)	2025
75	*Ch.*	Fo-kuo-yüan-wu-ch'an-shih-pi-yen-lu (佛果圜悟禪師碧巖録)	2003
	Eng.	The Blue Cliff Record	

Vol. No.		Title	*T.* No.
76-I	*Ch.*	I-pu-tsung-lun-lun (異部宗輪論)	2031
	Skt.	Samayabhedoparacanacakra	
	Eng.	The Cycle of the Formation of the Schismatic Doctrines	
76-II	*Ch.*	A-yü-wang-ching (阿育王經)	2043
	Skt.	Aśokarāja-sūtra (?)	
	Eng.	The Biographical Scripture of King Aśoka	
76-III	*Ch.*	Ma-ming-p'u-sa-ch'uan (馬鳴菩薩傳)	2046
	Eng.	The Life of Aśvaghoṣa Bodhisattva (In Lives of Great Monks and Nuns)	
76-IV	*Ch.*	Lung-shu-p'u-sa-ch'uan (龍樹菩薩傳)	2047
	Eng.	The Life of Nāgārjuna Bodhisattva (In Lives of Great Monks and Nuns)	
76-V	*Ch.*	P'o-sou-p'an-tou-fa-shih-ch'uan (婆藪槃豆法師傳)	2049
	Eng.	Biography of Dharma Master Vasubandhu (In Lives of Great Monks and Nuns)	
76-VI	*Ch.*	Pi-ch'iu-ni-ch'uan (比丘尼傳)	2063
	Eng.	Biographies of Buddhist Nuns (In Lives of Great Monks and Nuns)	
76-VII	*Ch.*	Kao-sêng-fa-hsien-ch'uan (高僧法顯傳)	2085
	Eng.	The Journey of the Eminent Monk Faxian (In Lives of Great Monks and Nuns)	
76-VIII	*Ch.*	Yu-fang-chi-ch'ao: T'ang-ta-ho-shang-tung-chêng-ch'uan (遊方記抄: 唐大和上東征傳)	2089-(7)
77	*Ch.*	Ta-t'ang-ta-tz'ŭ-ên-ssŭ-san-ts'ang-fa-shih-ch'uan (大唐大慈恩寺三藏法師傳)	2053
	Eng.	A Biography of the Tripiṭaka Master of the Great Ci'en Monastery of the Great Tang Dynasty	
78	*Ch.*	Kao-sêng-ch'uan (高僧傳)	2059
79	*Ch.*	Ta-t'ang-hsi-yü-chi (大唐西域記)	2087
	Eng.	The Great Tang Dynasty Record of the Western Regions	
80	*Ch.*	Hung-ming-chi (弘明集)	2102

Vol. No.	**Title**	***T.* No.**
81–92	*Ch.* Fa-yüan-chu-lin (法苑珠林)	2122
93-I	*Ch.* Nan-hai-chi-kuei-nei-fa-ch'uan (南海寄歸内法傳) *Eng.* Buddhist Monastic Traditions of Southern Asia	2125
93-II	*Ch.* Fan-yü-tsa-ming (梵語雑名)	2135
94-I	*Jp.* Shō-man-gyō-gi-sho (勝鬘經義疏)	2185
94-II	*Jp.* Yui-ma-kyō-gi-sho (維摩經義疏)	2186
95	*Jp.* Hok-ke-gi-sho (法華義疏)	2187
96-I	*Jp.* Han-nya-shin-gyō-hi-ken (般若心經秘鍵)	2203
96-II	*Jp.* Dai-jō-hos-sō-ken-jin-shō (大乘法相研神章)	2309
96-III	*Jp.* Kan-jin-kaku-mu-shō (觀心覺夢鈔)	2312
97-I	*Jp.* Ris-shū-kō-yō (律宗綱要) *Eng.* The Essentials of the Vinaya Tradition	2348
97-II	*Jp.* Ten-dai-hok-ke-shū-gi-shū (天台法華宗義集) *Eng.* The Collected Teachings of the Tendai Lotus School	2366
97-III	*Jp.* Ken-kai-ron (顯戒論)	2376
97-IV	*Jp.* San-ge-gaku-shō-shiki (山家學生式)	2377
98-I	*Jp.* Hi-zō-hō-yaku (秘藏寶鑰) *Eng.* The Precious Key to the Secret Treasury (In Shingon Texts)	2426
98-II	*Jp.* Ben-ken-mitsu-ni-kyō-ron (辨顯密二教論) *Eng.* On the Differences between the Exoteric and Esoteric Teachings (In Shingon Texts)	2427
98-III	*Jp.* Soku-shin-jō-butsu-gi (即身成佛義) *Eng.* The Meaning of Becoming a Buddha in This Very Body (In Shingon Texts)	2428
98-IV	*Jp.* Shō-ji-jis-sō-gi (聲字實相義) *Eng.* The Meanings of Sound, Sign, and Reality (In Shingon Texts)	2429

Vol. No.	Title	*T.* No.
98-V	*Jp.* Un-ji-gi （吽字義） *Eng.* The Meanings of the Word Hūṃ (In Shingon Texts)	2430
98-VI	*Jp.* Go-rin-ku-ji-myō-hi-mitsu-shaku （五輪九字明秘密釋） *Eng.* The Illuminating Secret Commentary on the Five Cakras and the Nine Syllables (In Shingon Texts)	2514
98-VII	*Jp.* Mitsu-gon-in-hotsu-ro-san-ge-mon （密嚴院發露懺悔文） *Eng.* The Mitsugonin Confession (In Shingon Texts)	2527
98-VIII	*Jp.* Kō-zen-go-koku-ron （興禪護國論）	2543
98-IX	*Jp.* Fu-kan-za-zen-gi （普勧坐禪儀）	2580
99–103	*Jp.* Shō-bō-gen-zō （正法眼藏）	2582
104-I	*Jp.* Za-zen-yō-jin-ki （坐禪用心記）	2586
104-II	*Jp.* Sen-chaku-hon-gan-nen-butsu-shū （選擇本願念佛集） *Eng.* Senchaku Hongan Nembutsu Shū	2608
104-III	*Jp.* Ris-shō-an-koku-ron （立正安國論） *Eng.* Risshōankokuron or The Treatise on the Establishment of the Orthodox Teaching and the Peace of the Nation (In Two Nichiren Texts)	2688
104-IV	*Jp.* Kai-moku-shō （開目抄） *Eng.* Kaimokushō or Liberation from Blindness	2689
104-V	*Jp.* Kan-jin-hon-zon-shō （觀心本尊抄） *Eng.* Kanjinhonzonsho or The Most Venerable One Revealed by Introspecting Our Minds for the First Time at the Beginning of the Fifth of the Five Five Hundred-year Ages (In Two Nichiren Texts)	2692
104-VI	*Ch.* Fu-mu-ên-chung-ching （父母恩重經）	2887

Vol. No.		Title	*T*. No.
105-I	*Jp.*	Ken-jō-do-shin-jitsu-kyō-gyō-shō-mon-rui (顯淨土眞實教行証文類)	2646
	Eng.	Kyōgyōshinshō: On Teaching, Practice, Faith, and Enlightenment	
105-II	*Jp.*	Tan-ni-shō (歎異抄)	2661
	Eng.	Tannishō: Passages Deploring Deviations of Faith	
106-I	*Jp.*	Ren-nyo-shō-nin-o-fumi (蓮如上人御文)	2668
	Eng.	Rennyo Shōnin Ofumi: The Letters of Rennyo	
106-II	*Jp.*	Ō-jō-yō-shū (往生要集)	2682
107-I	*Jp.*	Has-shū-kō-yō (八宗綱要)	蔵外
	Eng.	The Essentials of the Eight Traditions	
107-II	*Jp.*	San-gō-shī-ki (三教指帰)	蔵外
107-III	*Jp.*	Map-pō-tō-myō-ki (末法燈明記)	蔵外
	Eng.	The Candle of the Latter Dharma	
107-IV	*Jp.*	Jū-shichi-jō-ken-pō (十七條憲法)	蔵外